T0305759

UNCOVERING VALUE ADDED IN TRADE

New Approaches to Analyzing Global Value Chains

UNCOVERING VALUE ADDED IN TRADE

New Approaches to Analyzing Global Value Chains

Editor

Yuqing Xing

Asian Development Bank Institute, Japan

 World Scientific

NEW JERSEY · LONDON · SINGAPORE · BEIJING · SHANGHAI · HONG KONG · TAIPEI · CHENNAI

Published by

World Scientific Publishing Co. Pte. Ltd.

5 Toh Tuck Link, Singapore 596224

USA office: 27 Warren Street, Suite 401-402, Hackensack, NJ 07601

UK office: 57 Shelton Street, Covent Garden, London WC2H 9HE

Library of Congress Cataloging-in-Publication Data
Xing, Yuqing.
  Uncovering value added in trade new approaches to analyzing global value chains / by Yuqing Xing (Asian Development Bank Institute, Japan).
    pages cm
    ISBN 978-9814656351 (alk. paper)
    1. International trade. 2. International economic relations. I. Title.
    HF1379.X56 2015
    382--dc23
                          2015013437

British Library Cataloguing-in-Publication Data
A catalogue record for this book is available from the British Library.

In-house Editors: Prathima/Philly Lim

Typeset by Stallion Press
Email: enquiries@stallionpress.com

Printed in Singapore

Contents

List of Figures and Tables

Figures

Tables

Contributors

Christophe Degain is a Senior Statistical Officer in the International Trade Statistics Section at the World Trade Organization (WTO). He holds two Master's degrees (in Econometrics and in Enterprise Management) and a Postgraduate specialization in Statistics and Informatics from Paris University, France. He has been a certified project manager from the Project Management Institute since 2008. He joined the Organisation for Economic Co-operation and Development (OECD) in 1992 as a statistician in the Main Economic Indicators Division and moved to the WTO in 1996. In his current position, he conducts the development of statistical programs, such as trade in value added, and also leads information technology (IT) projects applied to statistics.

Galina Hale is a Research Advisor in the Economic Research Department at the Federal Reserve Bank of San Francisco. Her research focuses on International banking, bank regulation, international capital flows, and network analysis. Prior to joining the San Francisco Fed, she was an Assistant Professor in the Yale Economics Department, as well as a visiting Faculty member in the Stanford Economics Department and Haas Business School in Berkeley. She received her Ph.D. in Economics from the University of California, Berkeley, a Master's degree in Economics from the New Economic School in Moscow, and a Bachelor's degree in Economics from Moscow State University.

Bart Hobijn is a Senior Research Advisor in the Economic Research Department at the Federal Reserve Bank of San Francisco. He is an applied macroeconomist whose special interests are labor market dynamics, price measurement, and how technological progress contributes to economic growth. Prior to joining the San Francisco Fed, he was a Research Officer in the research and statistics group at the Federal Reserve Bank of New York. He completed his Master's degree in Econometrics at Erasmus University Rotterdam and his Ph.D. at New York University.

Satoshi Inomata is a Chief Senior Researcher at the Development Studies Center, Institute of Developing Economies, Japan External Trade Organization (IDE-JETRO). He received his Bachelor's degree in Politics and Economics from the University of London, a Master's in Development Economics from the University of Oxford, and his Ph.D. in Economics from Hitotsubashi University, Japan. He has been involved in the construction of the Asian International Input–Output Tables (AIOT) for 1990, 1995, and 2000.

Dr. Inomata's recent research includes in-depth studies of global value chains and trade in value added in the Asia-Pacific region using input–output techniques. In 2011, he co-edited and contributed to *Trade Patterns and Global Value Chains in East Asia*: *From Trade in Goods to Trade in Tasks*, a joint publication of the WTO and IDE-JETRO, which has been translated into five languages and disseminated worldwide. He is a member of the Council Board of the International Input–Output Association, the Editorial Board of Economic Systems Research, and the Editorial Board of the United Nations Handbook of Input–Output Table Compilation and Analysis.

Guoyong Liang is an Economic Affairs Officer at the United Nations Conference on Trade and Development (UNCTAD). He holds a Ph.D. in International Business from Rotterdam School of Management, Erasmus University. As one of the main authors of the annual flagship publication *World Investment Report* since 2005, he has accumulated ample experience and expertise in economic research, intergovernmental support, and technical cooperation.

Dr. Liang has published widely, with a focus on issues related to investment and development. He has done pioneering studies on the development impact of foreign direct investment at the industrial level, and his theoretical and empirical research has been recognized by the world's leading scholars as a major and unique contribution in the field of international investment. He is the author of *New Competition*: *Foreign*

Direct Investment and Industrial Development (Erasmus Research Institute of Management, 2004) and *Globalisation and Chinese Economy: The Next Three Decades* (forthcoming in 2015).

Andreas Maurer is the Chief of the International Trade Statistics Section at the WTO. He studied Economics with a specialization in Public Finance and Statistics/Econometrics at the University of Hohenheim and holds a doctorate in Economics. In 1990, he joined the United Nations Economic Commission for Europe (UNECE) and was editor-in-charge of its *Statistical Journal*. In 1994, he moved to the WTO. His current interests include measuring trade in services flows, especially mode 4, and trade in value added.

Bo Meng is a Research Fellow at the IDE-JETRO. He received his Ph.D. in Information Science from Tohoku University, Japan, in 2005. He was a visiting scholar at the OECD from 2009 to 2011 and at the United States International Trade Commission in 2013, carrying out joint research on global value chains. He has been an expert group member of the OECD Scientific Committee (Trade in Value Added) since 2012. His research interests include input–output analyses, CGE models, and low-carbon economics. He co-authored a chapter for the 2011 WTO and IDE-JETRO joint publication *Trade Patterns and Global Value Chains in East Asia*.

Yuqing Xing is a Professor of Economics of the National Graduate Institute for Policy Studies (GRIPS) in Tokyo. He served as the Director of the Capacity Building and Training Department of the Asian Development Bank Institute from September 2011 to August 2014. He has also held positions at the International University of Japan, the United Nations University World Institute for Development Economics Research as well as the Institute of Advanced Studies, and the National University of Singapore.

Dr. Xing's research focuses on international trade, FDI, exchange rates, and regional economic integration in Asia. He has published numerous articles in international refereed journals. His research on the iPhone and the Sino–US trade balance has been discussed widely in the mainstream media, challenging conventional views on bilateral trade statistics and instigating a reform of trade statistics. He earned his bachelor's and master's degrees from Peking University and received a Ph.D. in Economics from the University of Illinois at Urbana-Champaign.

Norihiko Yamano is responsible for the current edition of the harmonized input–output and related Inter-Country Input–Output Database (ICIO) at OECD. Various headline indicators such as Trade in Value Added (TiVA), carbon footprint, globalization, and jobs sustained by foreign demand are compiled by the ICIO model and reported in many international and academic meetings. He has also served in various external I–O and bilateral trade-related projects as a consortium member (e.g., EU FP7 WIOD) and external expert advisor (e.g., Japan IDE Asian IO, EU FP6 EXIOPOL, an EORA-hosted project, and CREEA). He has previously worked at the Central Research Institute of Electric Power Industry, Japan as a research economist, where he developed various types of economic models using originally developed regional public capital stock, labor force statistics, and interregional I–O tables.

Chapter 1

Introduction

Yuqing Xing

Modern international trade of manufacturing products is based on global value chains (GVCs). Many firms located in various countries are involved in production processes from product design, manufacturing parts, assembly, to distribution. The proliferation of GVCs has been integrating the world economy like an invisible hand. Supply chain trade differs from the trade observed by the British economist David Ricardo in a variety of aspects. As numerous countries are involved in producing a single product using imported intermediate inputs, gross trade values generally exaggerate export capacity and domestic import demand of nations, and this problem is particularly severe for countries specializing in final assembly (Xing and Detert 2010). Supply chain trade has transformed the relationship between trading nations from the traditional producer–consumer relations into partnerships, and bilateral trade relations have turned into multilateral ones.

Multinational enterprises (MNEs) are at the forefront of GVC growth. Innovation and outsourcing activities of MNEs have been performing a decisive role in creating and amplifying global trade. For instance, rising trade flows along value chains of iPhones are induced by technological innovations and outsourcing activities of Apple. Geographic trade patterns and bilateral trade balances have changed and are continuing to change dramatically with the proliferation of GVCs. Under supply chain trade, the national origins of traded goods are increasingly blurred. Rules of origin are the criteria used to determine the national source of a product, to implement trade measures and determine preferential treatment. However,

1

for goods produced within GVCs, it is difficult, and in many cases almost impossible, to define country origins. Further, the impact of exchange rates on bilateral trade balances is weakened. The currency appreciation of a country can only affect the value added generated by that country, not the whole value of the product. Besides, fluctuations of currencies of other countries participating in the same value chain either enhance or mitigate the impact. Protectionism is even more damaging to supply chain trade. Protection measures undermine the welfare of all countries involved in GVCs. The welfare reduction affects not only consumers, but also producers of the country imposing trade protection measures. Therefore, unilateral actions are not effective in solving bilateral imbalances.

To understand the distinctive features of value chain trade and the challenges to the principles of conventional trade rules, it is critical to introduce new trade statistics to trace the distribution of value added along GVCs. The Institute of Developing Economies, Japan External Trade Organization (IDE-JETRO), World Trade Organization (WTO), Organisation for Economic Co-operation and Development (OECD), and other institutions have begun the process of establishing a new global database on trade in value added. This book attempts to introduce and synthesize the frontier of the research on measuring trade in value added. It is a compilation of papers presented at the international conference "Production Networks, Value-Added, and Trade Statistics Reforms," held at Peking University in Beijing, People's Republic of China (PRC) in September 2012. The conference was jointly organized by the Asian Development Bank Institute (ADBI), IDE-JETRO, and the National School of Development of Peking University.

In Chapter 2, Christophe Degain and Andreas Maurer of the WTO discuss three issues: (i) factors driving the proliferation of GVCs, (ii) approaches to measuring trade flows within GVCs, and (iii) policy implications of GVCs for international trade and commercial policies. The authors point out that trade liberalization, foreign direct investment (FDI), pro-business policies, infrastructure development, and innovations in logistics services are principal forces facilitating the worldwide development of GVCs. Trade liberalization under the leadership of the WTO has significantly reduced tariffs on non-agricultural goods. In 2010, the average tariff of developed economies on non-agricultural goods was 2.5%, while that of developing countries was 8.4%. The sharp reduction in the tariff level substantially promoted cross-border flows of goods, which is essential for manufacturing goods along GVCs. MNEs generally lead GVCs and optimally allocate tasks of product design, manufacturing, assembly, and marketing across countries where GVCs are built and extended. The invention of standardized cargo containers has improved the efficiency of transportation and lowered the costs of moving intermediate inputs along GVCs.

The new trade paradigm unambiguously shows that conventional trade statistics are inconsistent with trade along GVCs. New trade statistics are needed to reflect actual contributions of countries participating in GVCs. The authors introduce three basic approaches to estimating trade flows taking place within GVCs: (i) case studies and microeconomic data, (ii) direct approaches by utilizing existing data on intermediate goods, and (iii) the indirect measurement of using international input–output tables. They also outline critical advantages and disadvantages of the three approaches. Case studies provide a clear sample of value added distribution over the tasks performed by economies. Compared with numerous goods traded in the global market, however, case studies cannot outline the overall picture of GVCs in global trade. The intermediate material approach faces the difficulty of distinguishing goods between intermediate and final uses. International input–output (II–O) tables trace origins and use of goods and services' inputs between countries and industries and can be used to analyze trade flows between both downstream and upstream partners of GVCs. It can also be linked with standard systems of national accounts. On the other hand, value added measurements derived with II–O tables are estimates, not actual values, and based on strong assumptions that the intensity of imported intermediate inputs is the same between production for domestic consumption and for exports.

Moreover, Degain and Maurer suggest that disaggregating trade into value added provides a new angle to measure service activities, bilateral trade balances, employment creation of international trade, and international competitiveness. Preliminary results of the WTO analysis cited in the chapter shows that the contribution of services in world trade would be doubled, while the trade surplus of Mexico with the United States (US) would be reduced by 35%. The authors show the geographical fragmentation of the Boeing 787 Dreamliner and argue that rules of origins are blurred in supply chain trade and "Made in the World" might be a better label for the country origin of goods manufactured along GVCs.

In Chapter 3, Norihiko Yamano of the OECD first briefly explains how inter-country input–output (ICIO) tables are constructed. The underlying data sources are national input–output tables, national accounts series, and estimated bilateral trade coefficients. The resulting ICIO tables include comprehensive information on international trade, consumption, investment, sales, and procurement by industries. Besides the application on trade policy, Yamano suggests that ICIO tables are useful in examining ecological footprints and the transmission mechanism of macroeconomic shocks. Unprecedented globalization and asymmetric stringency of environmental regulations among nations may lead to relocation of polluting industries from countries with strict oversight to countries with lenient environmental regulations. ICIO tables can be used to trace the movement of pollution such as carbon emissions due to FDI. The gross value of exports and imports are used in open macroeconomic models to gauge spillovers of domestic macroeconomic shocks to trading partners. In supply chain trade, imports contain a substantial portion of intermediate inputs required for producing exports, thus exaggerating domestic demand for foreign goods and services. The author suggests that value added in trade estimated with the ICIO tables would give rise to a better understanding on the transmission of macroeconomic shock spillovers.

Using ICIO tables to estimate value added in trade depends on the availability of national input–output tables and bilateral trade coefficients. It also requires strong assumptions, such as homothetic preferences and identical input bundles between domestic sales and exports. Questions arise as to how reliable the estimates are and whether they are acceptable with insignificant statistics errors. In Chapter 4, Yuqing Xing of National Graduate Institute for Policy Studies in Tokyo introduces a direct method to estimate trade in value added and applies the method to the case of the PRC. He finds that the domestic value added of the PRC's processing exports and processing high-tech exports gradually increased from 30% and 25% to 44% and 45%, respectively, during 1997–2012. On the other hand, the domestic content of processing exports with supplied materials over the same period fell to 14% from the peak level of 35%. By 2012, the domestic value added of the PRC's exports remained below 77%.

Xing's approach relies on aggregate data of imports used for manufacturing exports. Processing imports recorded by PRC customs usually do not include imported oil, natural gas, coal, and other minerals. Therefore, the estimates tend to overestimate domestic value added. However, they can be used as an upper limit to evaluate the reliability and accuracy of the estimates derived from ICIO tables. He compares the results with those of the OECD Trade in Value Added (TiVA) and finds that the latter significantly overestimates the domestic value added of the PRC's exports. In addition, Xing's analysis reveals that the time trend implied by the OECD TiVA is inconsistent with the fact that the share of processing exports decreased gradually as a proportion of the PRC's total exports. The assumption of homothetic preferences among consumers of the PRC's trading partners may be one of the reasons for the inconsistency, as the share of processing exports varies significantly between high- and low-income economies.

Production fragmentation has been analyzed extensively in the international trade literature. Currently, empirical studies measuring the intensity of production fragmentation have been lagging. For instance, vertical specialization indexes cannot provide a complete picture of the entire production chain, as they are not able to trace the sequence for more than two consecutive stages. In Chapter 5, Satoshi Inomata of IDE-JETRO proposes a new method to measure the magnitude of production fragmentation based on average propagation lengths: a technique of input–output analysis. The new measurement includes both direct and indirect linkages among sectors. Specifically, it captures all necessary indirect feedback occurring in a complete production process. Hence, the new approach covers every aspect of the vertical sequence in production fragmentation.

The author employs the Asian International Input–Output Table developed by IDE-JETRO and finds that the machinery, electronics, and automobile sectors have the highest level of production fragmentation among the 12 sectors investigated. The cross-country empirical analysis indicates that the participation in production fragmentation varies between countries, with Singapore, Malaysia, the Philippines, and Thailand having the highest fragmentation among the East Asian economies.

The PRC is the largest source of US imports. "Made in China" products are available in all corners of the US market. The PRC firms perform only a part of the tasks in the GVCs where the US is the destination market. US firms provide the necessary retail logistics and transportation services for delivering these products to US consumers and businesses. Therefore, a part of the US consumption of such products goes to locally produced services. In Chapter 6, Galina Hale and Bart Hobijn of the US Federal Reserve Bank apply input–output tables to evaluate the share of imports and commodities in US consumption and investment. They conclude that 82% of expenditures by US consumers go to goods that are entirely produced domestically. Furthermore, 55% of consumer spending on goods labeled "Made in China" actually covers the costs of the domestic wholesale, transportation, and retail components. Hence, only 1.9% of the consumer spending reflects the costs of the goods imported from the PRC. In the same fashion, the authors find that 20% of US private fixed investment spending goes to imported goods, of which 4.2% goes to imports from the PRC. Despite the advent of unprecedented globalization, the US economy remains relatively closed.

Most studies on GVCs focus on cross-country production fragmentation. The sheer size and diversity of regional economies in the PRC imply that the regional economies may be integrated with domestic value chains (DVCs). In Chapter 7, Bo Meng of IDE-JETRO extends existing studies on GVCs to DVCs and estimates domestic trade in value added by using the interregional input–output tables of the PRC. The domestic trade in value added is defined as one region's value added induced by another region's final demand. The empirical analysis indicates that the regional value added of the PRC's north coast exports to the southwest region accounted for 94% in 2002, while those of the east coast to the south coast was only 40%. From 2002 to 2007, shares of value added decreased for all regions, suggesting improvement in the participation of regional value chains and further enhancement in domestic market integration. The author also employs the estimates of domestic trade in value added to examine revealed comparative advantages, as gross trade flows generally lead to distortions of measuring regional comparative advantage.

In Chapter 8, Guoyong Liang of the United Nations Conference on Trade and Development has coined the term *"Fox–Apple"* to represent their inter-firm relations. Foxconn is the exclusive assembler of iPhones and iPads, invented and owned by Apple. The author argues that the *Fox–Apple* alliance shows distinctive features of GVCs: (i) the cooperation is "born global" rather than the result of an evolution process from vertical integration, to domestic subcontracting, and eventually to foreign contract manufacturing; (ii) it is a partnership between two leading firms at two key stages of the value chain — product design and manufacturing; and (iii) "Global Value Tree" may be a better interpretation of the GVC value chain defined by *Fox–Apple*. In the tree representation, the top is the distribution network controlled by Apple, the middle is Foxconn, and the bottom is the production network — suppliers connected to Foxconn. FDI and contract manufacturing are the two foremost channels through which GVCs are formed. He argues that *Fox–Apple* is a typical example of contract manufacturing.

The studies in this book suggest that conventional trade statistics are not suitable for analyzing trade under GVCs. Tracing trade in value added is crucial for a better understanding of the fundamental changes brought by GVCs. Many issues such as bilateral trade balances, revealed comparative advantage, and rules of origin require re-examination in the context of GVCs. International input–output tables provide a convenient tool to measure trade in value added. However, the results of II–O tables are the estimates derived with strong attached assumptions. Caution is warranted in utilizing the data for analytical studies.

Reference

Xing, Y. and N. Detert. 2010. How the iPhone Widens the United States Trade Deficit with the People's Republic of China. ADBI Working Paper No. 257. Tokyo: Asian Development Bank Institute.

Chapter 2

Implications of Global Value Chains for Trade Statistics and Trade Policy

*Christophe Degain and Andreas Maurer**

The last three decades saw the creation and intensification of global value chains due to changed business models. Today, the production of final goods often requires performing several tasks across countries. This chapter describes the factors that have led to "trade in tasks" and explains the biases of traditional trade statistics in depicting this new trade reality. Approaches to correct these biases by estimating trade in value added are described with their respective statistical challenges. Changing the perspective from a "gross" reporting to a "value added" angle has implications on trade indicators. Some common considerations are revisited, such as the importance of services, interpretation of trade balance, export competitiveness, and risks associated with increased interdependencies between economies. Traditional rules and principles may also be put into question. The chapter concludes with some directions for trade policy to foster participation in global value chains.

2.1. Introduction

Technological progress, reduced transportation costs, and market-opening incentives have all contributed to build a new business model, leading to the development of globally integrated value chains (Figure 2.1). Mass consumption, mainly in industrialized countries, matches with production capacity in developing countries. This development has had a marked impact on international trade statistics and has also influenced the revision of international statistical standards such as the Balance of Payments (BOP) and the System of National Accounts (SNA). Trade indicators, derived

---

*This chapter represents the opinions of the authors and is the product of professional research. It is not meant to represent the position or opinions of the World Trade Organization (WTO) or its members, nor the official position of any staff member.

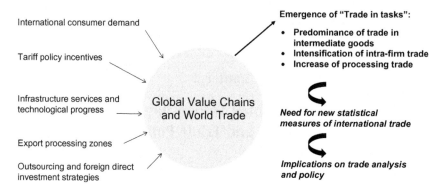

Figure 2.1. Global value chains and world trade — ins and outs.
Source: World Trade Organization.

either from customs statistics or other statistical frames, also need to be reinterpreted.

This chapter outlines several topics that are explored within the "Made in the World" initiative (MIWI) launched by the World Trade Organization (WTO) in 2011.[1] It also exploits preliminary findings from the Trade in Value Added (TiVA) database released jointly by the Organisation for Economic Co-operation and Development (OECD) and WTO on 16 January 2013.[2]

First, this chapter examines the global value chains (GVCs)[3] phenomenon, its origins, and repercussions on international trade statistics. Second, it describes the tools and methodology applied to measure trade in value added. Third, it presents indicators in value added terms and their potential use for trade policy. Fourth, it illustrates some WTO rules and principles in the GVC context. The last part of the chapter outlines some trade policy directions for promoting GVCs.

---

[1] See MIWI website at http://www.wto.org/miwi.

[2] The OECD–WTO TiVA database is accessible at http://stats.oecd.org/Index.aspx? DataSetCode=TIVA_OECD_WTO.

[3] A "value chain" represents the sequence of productive activities that firms undertake to create value, including the various production steps but also all activities belonging to the demand chain/client side such as marketing, sales, or customer service. The term "global value chains" stands for value chains that are composed of multiple firms spread across several countries.

2.2. The Rise of Global Value Chains: Why and What Impact?

2.2.1. *Factors that led to the development of global value chains*

Improved market access stimulates trade and the setup of GVCs. Import tariffs constitute the backbone of trade policy and were central in all rounds of General Agreement on Tariffs and Trade (GATT)/WTO negotiations. Table 2.1 presents the evolution of tariffs applied to industrial products, by level of economic development as of 2000. Historically, tariffs applied to manufacturing goods have decreased significantly in developed economies. Even though the average rate of applied tariffs on manufacturing goods had already reached low levels in 2000, it still decreased during the last decade.[4] A similar downward trend can be observed for developing economies and least-developed countries (LDCs).

Freer trade is intrinsically an incentive for the development of GVCs, but low tariffs on intermediate goods,[5] exchanged within supply chains, are even more conducive to their expansion. Accordingly, Figure 2.2 highlights that tariffs on semi-processed goods were lower in Asia in 2011 compared to either raw materials or processed products. For some economies, such as the Republic of Korea and Thailand, they were less than a third of those applied to raw materials, which is a clear stimulus for the development of

Table 2.1. Evolution of applied tariffs on non-agricultural goods, by level of economic development, 2000–2011 (%).

Economic category	2000 AV tariffs only	2005 or 2006 AV + AVEs	2010 or 2011 AV + AVEs
Developed economies	3.4	2.9	2.5
Developing economies	9.5	9.2	8.4
Least-developed countries	—	13.1	11.5

Notes: An *ad valorem* (AV) tariff is a customs tariff duty, expressed as a percentage of the value of the imported good. An *AV equivalent* (AVE) is an estimate of a tariff, expressed as a percentage of the value of the imported good.
Source: World Trade Organization, integrated database and world tariff profiles.

---

[4]"Non-agricultural goods" are assumed to be a proxy of manufacturing goods.
[5]Intermediate goods are inputs (parts, components, and accessories) used for the production of other goods.

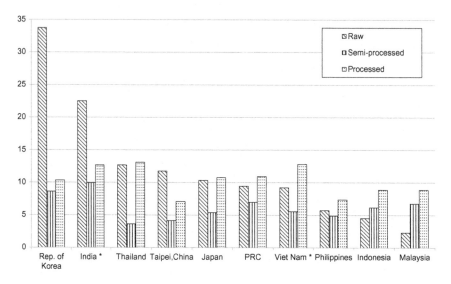

Figure 2.2. Tariff escalation in selected Asian economies, 2011 (%).

Notes: "Raw" products include agricultural and food products. *Data for 2010, PRC = People's Republic of China.

Source: World Trade Organization, integrated database.

GVCs.[6] Actual tariff escalation[7] can only be observed for a few economies, such as Indonesia and Malaysia. However, progressive application of low tariffs can be partially offset by non-tariff measures (NTMs) such as licensing, quantity controls, phytosanitary measures, and antidumping, to which governments resort to limit imports.

Companies' outsourcing and foreign direct investment (FDI) strategies also play a substantial role in the shift toward international production networks. Search for cost savings and production efficiency leads companies to make strategic choices on outsourcing some of their non-core

---

[6]The "raw material" category is not homogeneous. In particular, agricultural and food products usually benefit from a much higher nominal protection than other commodities such as minerals or fuels, which are used as inputs by the industries (see Diakantoni and Escaith 2012).

[7]Tariff escalation refers to the situation where import duties on raw materials are the lowest, and move progressively higher on intermediate or semi-processed goods upward to the finished goods.

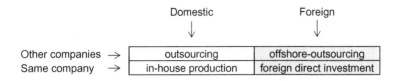

Figure 2.3. Typology of companies' outsourcing and offshoring strategies.
Source: World Trade Organization.

activities. Outsourcing (short for "outside resource using") is extensively used by manufacturing and services industries. When dealing with GVCs, the strategic choice relates to offshore-outsourcing (or offshoring) for companies to profit from comparative advantages (in labor cost, technical skills, and natural resources) in other countries and foreign industries (Figure 2.3).

International fragmentation of production and offshoring of inputs and business functions also stem from the increasing sophistication of inputs and technologies used for producing goods, which entails multiple production steps. Each company becomes specialized in the production of a specific component or activity, which relates to the notion of trade in tasks.

FDI policies of multinational enterprises (MNEs) involved in GVCs usually aim to optimize their production process to benefit from comparative advantages of partner countries and companies. Through FDI, MNEs invest in foreign productive assets, by acquiring or taking an active participation in the management of a foreign company. Nowadays, companies invest abroad not only in the manufacturing or the construction sector but also in services, as they can offshore parts of their business functions. The customs authorities of the People's Republic of China (PRC) provide processing trade data broken down by type of enterprise, that is, state-owned enterprises and foreign-invested enterprises, which gives an idea of the effect of GVCs on the PRC's trade. Table 2.2 shows that 83.6% of the PRC's processing trade in 2011 relied on companies managed by foreign investors.

Within supply chains, materials need to be stored and moved from original suppliers to final consumers. This is why infrastructure and logistics

Table 2.2. Exports from the People's Republic of China by type of trade and enterprise, 2000, 2005, and 2011.

	2000	2005	2011
Total exports ($ billion)	249	762	1,899
Total processing exports	138	417	836
of which:			
State-owned enterprises (SOE)	37	47	64
Foreign-invested enterprises (FIE)	97	347	699
Other enterprises	4	23	73
Processing exports (FIE)/Total processing exports (%)	70.3	83.2	83.6
Total processing exports/Total exports (%)	55.4	54.7	44.0

Source: PRC customs statistics.

services are a prerequisite for the development and competitiveness of GVCs. They play a key role in lowering trade costs and smoothing the overall functioning of GVCs. For example, the invention of the container changed not only international transportation but also the management and organization of international trade and production. Millions of containers cross the oceans every year, carrying almost 90% of world trade in volume terms. The total container trade volume was estimated at 151 million TEUs[8] in 2011, about 1.4 billion tons.

Improvement of administrative and customs procedure, a key part of trade facilitation advocated by the WTO, as well as technological progress (such as the internet or mobile technology) are crucial for the development of GVCs. Additionally, economies like Singapore and Hong Kong, China, which developed excellent logistics services, are major actors in world production chains and trade as they provide storage services and redistribute inputs and final goods among GVCs through their re-exports activity.

Setting up business-friendly policies with favorable trading conditions is of high importance for the expansion of supply chains. Export processing zones (EPZs) symbolize such proactive programs as they gather factors discussed above, such as tax and FDI incentives, as well as appropriate transport and logistics infrastructure, combined with either a specialized or

---

[8]TEU stands for "twenty-foot equivalent unit," the measure used for capacity in container transportation.

low-cost labor force. EPZs are earmarked areas with special administrative and fiscal status dedicated to the promotion of trade and investment. The world's first EPZ was created in Ireland at Shannon Airport in the 1950s. Since then, EPZs have spread all over the world and often represent a starting point for emerging economies to integrate global production and trade. In some cases, EPZs developed tremendously and largely contribute to the export performance of an economy.

2.2.2. *Trade in tasks*

All these factors and the resulting expansion of GVCs led to changes in the nature of world trade. The notion of "trade in tasks" emerged (WTO and IDE-JETRO 2011), corresponding to the distribution of activities performed by companies within GVCs. Nowadays, intermediate goods drive world trade. In 2011, they represented 55% of world non-fuel merchandise exports. In other words, a large part of world merchandise trade takes place within GVCs.

Intra-firm trade represents exchanges taking place between parent companies and their foreign affiliates created through FDI. The fragmentation of production across countries and the vertical integration of MNEs have increased the weight of intra-firm transactions in world trade. For instance, 20% of US merchandise exports and 28% of US exports of private services (Figure 2.4) relied on intra-firm transactions in 2011.

Today, numerous manufactured goods consumed all over the world are produced in export processing zones. In 2010, 20% of merchandise exports from developing economies came out of processing zones (estimate based on the BoP). Moreover, as shown in Table 2.2, the PRC's processing activity, mainly carried out in coastal provinces, represented 44% of its total exports in 2011.

2.2.3. *The implications of trade in tasks*

The evolution of international trade patterns has repercussions on trade statistics and on trade policy. On the statistical side, changed economic and trade environments caused the revision of international statistical concepts applied for the collection and compilation of official statistics, such as the BoP and the SNA. For example, the recent sixth edition of the BoP manual, which provides guidance to national BoP compilers, revised the treatment of

C. Degain & A. Maurer

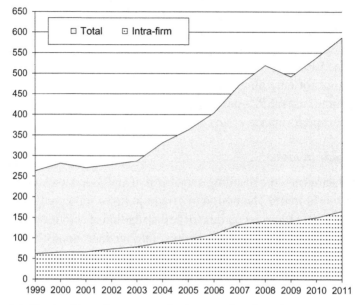

Figure 2.4. Total and intra-firm exports of private services from the United States, 1999–2011 ($ million).

Source: Bureau of Economic Analysis, US Department of Commerce.

goods for processing to better reflect exchanges that happen within global production processes. When there is no change of ownership within the international transaction, the "goods sent abroad for processing" are now excluded from the goods account. Instead, the new manual recommends that processing fee is recorded under "manufacturing services on physical inputs owned by others." On the other hand, customs-based merchandise trade statistics use the physical crossing of a border as a basic principle to record international transactions. It still records merchandise flows falling under the "goods for processing" regime but saw the addition of data elements such as mode of transport or country of consignment which help better trace goods in GVCs.

Nevertheless, even with these revisions, measuring the development of trade related to global production arrangements is a challenge. Conventional trade statistics do not show the real picture of international trade in a globalized economy. For example, the "country of origin" recorded for imports is often the last country in the production chain, which does not reflect geographical fragmentation of the manufacturing process. The transaction value assigned to this last country of origin is overstated, since other contributors (origins) to the product are totally ignored. Another bias observed with conventional trade statistics is the multiple counting of gross value of intermediate goods when they cross borders a number of times. That is, the value of the components or accessories used to create final goods are counted once they are initially exported but also each time they cross borders as they are embedded in more refined products.

Thus, the emergence of trade in tasks calls for new ways of measuring and analyzing trade. This is why the WTO Statistics Group embarked on a project to measure trade in value added terms, in close cooperation with the OECD and other partners like IDE-JETRO, the United States International Trade Commission (USITC), and the World Input–Output Database (WIOD) project team. The main benefits expected from the new approach are to circumvent biases faced by conventional trade statistics, to better evaluate the actual contribution of foreign trade to an economy, to take into account the interconnection of national economies within global production chains, and to better assess the impact of the services sector on trade.

The WTO "Made in the World" initiative (MIWI) encompasses all WTO efforts in the area of trade in value added. The core ideas behind MIWI are to constitute a forum for discussion and exchange of experiences, to provide links to relevant information and statistics that mirror trade relations as they truly exist today, and to foster the development of statistical methodologies for compiling trade in value added indicators as well as to promote a better integration of statistical data "silos" (e.g., business, trade, finance, and employment statistics).

Another objective of MIWI is to highlight the implications of GVCs on trade policy and negotiations. For example, since a country's exports often contain inputs imported from partner countries, import duties may in fact tax one's own exports.[9] Another example relates to bilateral trade imbalances; the surpluses or deficits relying on products created within international supply chains are not the same when considering the value added method. For example, the trade deficit of US with the PRC is reduced by about

---

[9]For more details, see Section 2.4.

25% in 2009 when measured in value added rather than with the traditional statistical measure.

The conduct of effective trade policy and government policy in general requires knowledge of where value added comes from. In that respect, the trade in value added approach brings new perspectives for trade analysis. At the same time, trade policy needs to be adapted to business reality. Such policy aspects are further explored in Section 2.4.

2.3. Trade in Value Added: Measuring Trade in a Globalized World

2.3.1. *Three approaches to measure trade taking place within global value chains*

2.3.1.1. *Case studies and microeconomic data*

Case studies look at a specific product or firm and trace the value created along the various steps in the design, production, and distribution of a manufactured good. Several studies have illustrated the trade in value added concept through Apple's emblematic devices, first on the iPod (Linden *et al.* 2007), the iPhone 3G (Xing and Detert 2010), and then the iPad/iPhone 4 (Kraemer *et al.* 2011). Earlier examples of such studies included the global process for producing Texas Instrument high-speed chips (Burrows 1995) and Mattel Barbie dolls (Tempest 1996).

Although case studies provide a better understanding of the global industrial model that lies behind trade in value added, they do not cover a representative sample of international trade.[10] Micro data may also help to bypass some constraints faced with input–output analysis, such as the assumption of homogeneity of enterprises. National statistical institutes in some developed and emerging countries are also undertaking specific firm surveys in order to trace the source and localization of value added. These surveys are used to complement traditional trade and business statistics and allow for a better picture of supply chains and impute more adequately the domestic part of value added.

---

[10]There are some exceptions, when most manufacturing exports are undertaken in export processing zones, such as for the PRC and Mexico. In such a case, the survey can make use of available administrative registers in order to provide representative estimates.

2.3.1.2.   *Use of existing data on trade in intermediate goods*: *The direct measurement*

A direct measure of the domestic value added contained in exports may consist of subtracting all imported intermediate goods from total exports. Trade in intermediate goods reflects the evolution of intra- and inter-industry activity and is a proxy of transactions taking place within GVCs. It is usually measured through a breakdown of trade statistics according to the UN classification of Broad Economic Categories (BEC).[11] The difficulty with this approach is that some goods can be either intermediate or final depending on their use.[12] Another limitation is that the BEC classification is limited to goods, and there is no similar classification for services.

2.3.1.3.   *The use of international input–output (II–O) tables*: *The indirect measurement*

An alternative method to measure trade in value added relies on the use of international input–output (II–O) tables. II–O tables gather national I–O tables and bilateral trade data on goods and services into a consistent statistical framework. This approach is often referred to as the indirect measure, as the results obtained are not based on actual value added figures but rather derived from a combination of various statistical sources.

II–O tables have been retained by the WTO for compilation of trade in value added. The main II–O tables currently used by the WTO are sourced from IDE-JETRO (AIO table), OECD (ICIO table), and the WIOD project (WIOT table).

The most effective component of these tables is the intermediate demand matrix, which describes the origin and use of goods and services' inputs produced and exchanged between the countries and industries covered by the table. Thus, II–O tables provide an advantage with regard to conventional trade statistics, since they inform on the sectoral use and destination of imported intermediates. The use of II–O tables has

---

[11]The BEC classification defines three classes of goods: intermediate, capital, and consumption goods. From a national account perspective, capital and consumption goods are intended for final use.

[12]See Sturgeon and Memedovic (2011).

several practical advantages. They are based on publicly available statistical information (trade, national accounts, and national I–O tables). Moreover, as II–O tables are linked to the system of national accounts, it allows for many downstream analyses and relates the value added trade within GVCs to other macroeconomic variables, such as sectoral effective protection, labor content of trade, and environmental impact.

The construction of II–O tables presents some constraints and limitations which need to be considered when interpreting the results obtained. For example, it is presumed that, for a given country and sector, all firms use the same goods and services (or inputs) to produce the same outputs. Another strong assumption refers to the homogeneity of enterprises working for the domestic or the export sector. In other words, the intensity in the use of imported inputs is assumed to be the same between production for exports or for domestic consumption. However, in reality, there can be a large difference between domestic and export-oriented firms, especially in developing countries and economies where processing trade is prevalent. This may lead to the domestic value added content of exports to be strongly overvalued. Another limitation is about the timeliness of national I–O tables which are only available for some base years, usually every five years, which may affect the analytical relevancy of the years in between since no corresponding production structure is available. To overcome this weakness, procedures can be used to update I–O technical coefficients outside of benchmark years (such as the RAS method). Finally, II–O tables are only available for a limited number of aggregated sectors (e.g., 37 sectors for the OECD ICIO tables and 35 sectors for the WIOD table) and thus are not suited for an analysis of trade in value added at the product level.

The above remarks confirm that the evaluation of trade in value added through II–O tables is indirect and the fact that obtained figures are estimates rather than actual measures.

2.3.2. *The statistical methodology — basic principles*

Over the last years, several research initiatives took place to develop statistical methodologies to estimate trade in value added terms. The notion of vertical specialization, or foreign content of exports, developed by Hummels *et al.* (2001) was at the origin of a series of research papers aiming at estimating "value added trade," including Daudin *et al.* (2011) and Johnson and Noguera (2012). The USITC[13] developed these concepts further into a consistent framework enabling full decomposition of a country's gross exports by its various value added components. The members of the WIOD project team also completed methodological research to estimate the factor content of trade with links to capital and labor income (e.g., Los *et al.* 2012; Stehrer 2012).

The methodologies applied for estimating trade in value added exploit the various elements of the II–O table. Figure 2.5 illustrates the basic elements which compose an II–O table. The intermediate demand matrix includes all the inputs consumed to produce the output. It shows the interaction between country-sectors that supply intermediate goods or services (rows of the matrix) and the ones that receive and use them (columns of the matrix) to produce other goods or services. The final demand matrix contains the consumption in final goods from households and governments as well as industry investment and variation of stocks. The value added and gross output vectors are available for each country-sector of origin.

The imports and exports of each country-sector are obtained through the respective sums of rows and columns from the intermediate and final demand matrices, excluding domestic transactions.

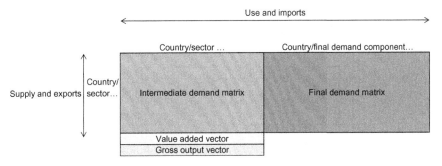

Figure 2.5. The basic components of II–O tables.
Source: World Trade Organization.

---

[13] See Koopman *et al.* (2012).

The input–output analysis is closely associated to the application of the Leontief inverse matrix L which can be expressed in mathematical terms as $L = (I - A)^{-1}$, where I represents the identity matrix and A the technical coefficients matrix (ratios of intermediate inputs used for the production on output by country-sector of origin and destination). Each element of L represents the inputs directly and indirectly (inputs required to produce other inputs) provided by producing country-sector to generate one unit of final demand in the destination country/sector. The concept of the Leontief inverse matrix is of high interest for trade in value added analysis as it gives information on the backward linkages between countries and sectors; in other words, it takes into account the various steps that occur among the international production chains.

The various methodologies using II–O tables to estimate trade in value added terms rely on the same core matrix, which combines the Leontief inverse matrix and a value added ratio based on the II–O table, or $V * L$, where V is the direct value added coefficients' vector corresponding to the ratio of direct domestic value added on total output (see the last two rows in Figure 2.5). The $V * L$ matrix reflects the production structure depicted in the II–O table, expressed in value added terms (Figure 2.6). It contains all the value added coefficients by country-sector of origin and destination which are applied to estimate trade in net terms. Each element of the $V * L$

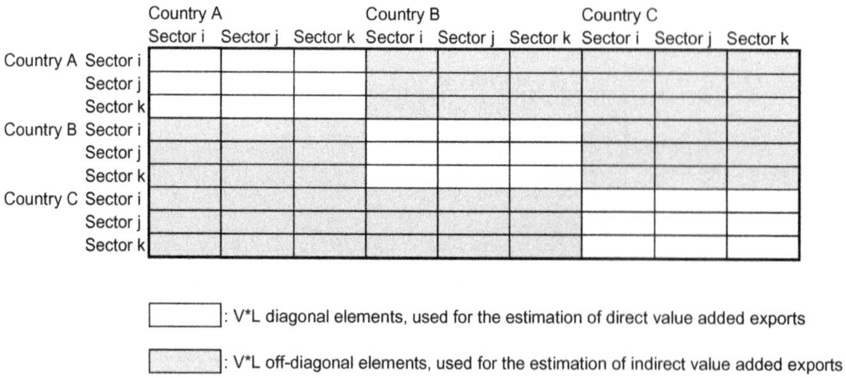

Figure 2.6. Schematic presentation of the $V * L$ matrix, based on II–O table with three countries and sectors.

Source: World Trade Organization.

matrix represents the domestic value added share of all inputs produced by a country-sector (rows of the matrix) and used either within the country itself or by another country-sector (columns of the matrix).

The white cells in Figure 2.6 contain the intra-country value added coefficients applied to estimate the domestic value added content directly consumed[14] by partner/importing countries (see indicator 1 below). The grey cells contain the inter-country coefficients to consider when estimating the indirect (see indicators 2 and 3), and foreign (see indicator 4) value added components of gross exports.

The main indicators obtained from the application of the $V * L$ coefficients matrix to a gross exports vector (Figure 2.7) are the following:

Indicator 1: *Domestic value added directly consumed by the importing country.* This corresponds to the value added sent abroad and directly absorbed by the partner country.

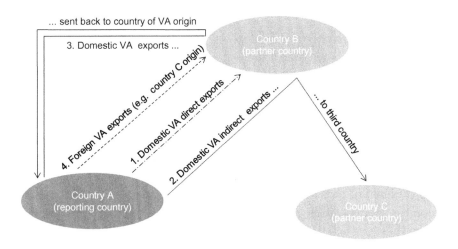

Figure 2.7. The main value added components of gross exports.

Note: VA = Value added

Source: World Trade Organization.

---

[14]On a terminological aspect, since the value added in question refers not only to the value contained in goods and services but also to that included in investment, which is a component of final demand, one could rather say "absorbed" instead of "consumed." While goods and services are "consumed," investment is rather "absorbed" by public entities and enterprises.

Indicator 2: *Domestic value added contained in intermediates exported to a partner country which re-exports it to a third country, embodied in other goods or services.* This can be referred to as indirect value added exports, as the exported goods or services are not directly consumed by the importing country. To some extent, this illustrates the length and characteristic of the value added path within international production chains.

Indicator 3: *Domestic value added of exported intermediates which are sent back to the country of value added origin.* This corresponds to the value which is finally re-imported embodied in other goods or services. This indicator may also be considered as a special case of value added re-exports, where the third country is the same as the first exporter.

Indicator 4: *Foreign value added of exports.* This corresponds to the value added of inputs imported to produce intermediate or final goods or services to be exported. When expressed as a share of gross exports, it corresponds to "vertical specialization" as developed by Hummels *et al.* (2001).

The sum of these four indicators, or value added components of gross exports, matches exactly the gross exports figures as officially reported.

2.3.3. *The statistical challenges*

For a relevant and continuing analysis of trade in value added terms, international or global I–O tables that cover a set of reporting countries along with an estimate of the "rest of the world" are indispensable. Since they rely on the provision of national I–O tables, development and improvement of the latter has to be considered a priority. The first aspect concerns data availability. Major economies produce I–O tables on a regular basis. However, smaller economies, especially from Africa and the Middle East, provide scarce information or no I–O tables at all. Improving country coverage of II–O tables is important to better assess the role played by small economies in GVCs and to address development-related questions. Additionally, I–O tables would require further standardization, for example regarding adoption of standard industrial classifications, to facilitate their reconciliation within an international statistical framework.

Once national I–O tables are made available, II–O tables gather and link them through the use of bilateral trade statistics and estimates, by industry and end-use category. However, bilateral trade statistics face some availability and consistency issues, which require improvements in many areas.

One characteristic of international trade statistics is that they are compiled by national sources independently from their trading counterparts. Consequently, country A exports to country B do not always match country B imports from country A. There are many reasons for such asymmetry (e.g., CIF or FOB trade valuation method, time gaps, triangular trade, exchange rates, and confidentiality concerns), which directly affects the relevancy of II–O tables. Another challenge for trade statistics is to improve the sectoral coverage of bilateral data on trade in services. The latter is most often available only at the total level without sectoral breakdown. This is obviously an issue for the construction of II–O tables, and estimation methods of bilateral and sectoral trade in services need to be improved.

Getting quality bilateral trade statistics is necessary but not sufficient for II–O table construction. Indeed, I–O tables require information on the use of the imported goods or services, including both type of end use (intermediate or final consumption or investment) and the sector which receives the goods. However, conventional trade data do not provide any information on sectoral destination of imported goods or services, which therefore has to be estimated within the construction of I–O tables. Assumption techniques exist but the tools applied for estimating the use of imported goods and services can be enhanced. This is one reason the OECD has started developing a bilateral trade database by industry and end-use category to support *inter alia* the production of II–O tables.

From a systemic perspective, the trade in value added program inserts itself naturally into the international statistical system, by using and reinforcing synergies between the macro perspective (SNA and BoP) and economic statistics (trade, production, and labor). It is therefore a vehicle for closer inter-agency cooperation. In this context, the WTO is cooperating closely with the OECD and other stakeholders, such as IDE-JETRO, USITC, and the former WIOD project group, to establish a common methodology to compile official trade indicators in value added terms. But measuring trade in value added is more difficult than measuring trade in gross terms, as many statistical and methodological issues remain to be solved. This is why international efforts and cooperation should keep the momentum going with the objective to establish best practices for I–O table compilation, to address methodological issues on trade in value added, and to define relevant indicators to assist trade policy and negotiations.

2.4.   A New Angle for Trade Analysis and Policy

2.4.1.   *Increasing role of manufacturing and business services in world trade*

Global or regional production networks are made up of a web of supply chains, with services as the glue that holds these webs together. Without communication, financing, or logistics, it would be impossible for these supply chains to complement each other and operate efficiently. Besides, manufacturing is no more just about making goods with machines and use of technology through the production and assembly stages. Services are increasingly used as inputs within the production phase itself, especially within GVCs, as they establish the links between the successive operations taking place in various factories and countries.

In its broadest sense, the production process starts with business services such as research and development, design, and marketing. Service activities take place before, during, and after the actual production of goods. This has led to the advent of new term "manu-services" developed by Sissons (2011), which represents all activities that combine manufacturing goods with services. Manu-services include a simple combination of goods with complementary services (such as maintenance and installation) to complex integration of manufacturing and services (which may involve producing services such as development, design, and after-sales care in close integration with the production of a good) (Sissons 2011). Another study from the Swedish Board of Trade (2010) referred to the prominence of services in the manufacturing sector as "servicification," meaning that manufacturing (also agricultural) industries tend to produce, buy, sell, and export more and more services.

The inventory of services in current production chains would not be complete without mentioning customer services, which often come along with the product bought by the final consumer. Indeed, companies no longer sell standalone goods, they instead set up whole packages combining their products with services. This is the case with "after sales" services (e.g., installation or implementation assistance, client support, and technical maintenance), which constitute an increasing share of the price of exported goods. The rise of customer services fostered the development of "services supply chains" aiming to efficiently organize IT infrastructure and logistics among a network of companies with the objective to meet the increasing variety of customer expectations without excessive costs or response time.

Services contribute predominantly, sometimes more than physical inputs, to the value added contained in goods produced within supply chains and traded all over the world. The compilation of trade in value added terms enables breakdown of value added of trade flows by sector and a more accurate estimate of the actual contribution of services in the value added export of an economy. Indeed, with merchandise trade statistics, the value of the services used in the production process or associated to the final product is diluted within the commercial value of the goods reported to customs.

As shown in Figure 2.8, when measured in value added terms, the world average contribution of services is twice as high. This has important implications for industrial and trade policies, especially those related to competitiveness, integration of small and medium-sized enterprises (SMEs) in global value chains, and the relationship between trade and employment

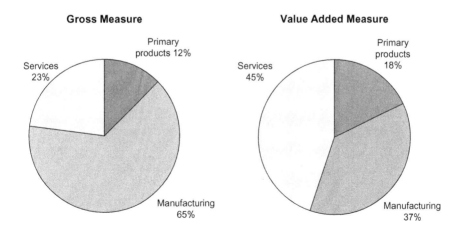

Figure 2.8. World exports by main sector aggregate, 2008.

Source: World Trade Organization estimates based on Organisation for Economic Co-operation and Development inter-country input–output table.

(see Section 2.4.3), since nowadays most labor is concentrated in the services sector.

Interestingly, Figure 2.9 highlights that a similar share of services value added may be embedded in the manufactured products exported by

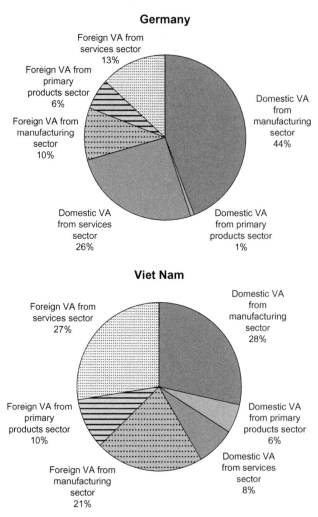

Figure 2.9. Shares of domestic and foreign sectoral value added contributions to exports of manufactured products, 2008.

Source: World Trade Organization estimates based on Organisation for Economic Co-operation and Development inter-country input–output table.

a developed economy (Germany, 39%), and an emerging one (Viet Nam, 35%). The difference lies in the proportion of domestic and foreign services. While two-thirds of the manufacturing services used to produce German manufacturing exports are of national origin, it is only 23% for Viet Nam, which relies much more on foreign services providers.

2.4.2. *Bilateral trade balances revisited*

Bilateral trade balances, and more especially deficits, usually draw attention of trade policy makers. However, surpluses or deficits that rely on manufactured goods produced within global supply chains are not the same when considering the value added approach. Conventional trade statistics, reported in gross terms, mask the origins of intermediate inputs and thus skew bilateral trade balances. The value added measure modifies balances for a number of countries, as it allocates value added according to the actual contribution of each economy in the production chain. This is demonstrated in Figure 2.10, which presents four economies' bilateral trade balances for 2008, measured in gross and in value added terms. Both goods and services are included, and balances are shown with respect to five selected partners. The PRC's trade surplus with the US is reduced by around 27% when measured in value added, and its counterpart. The US commercial deficit *vis-à-vis* the PRC, is obviously reduced in the same proportion which stresses that the value added approach can help to reconsider trade policies focusing on bilateral shortfalls. Similarly, Mexico's trade surplus with the US would decrease by about 35% with the value added measure. For both countries, the reason for such a reduction is the presence of EPZs that usually import inputs, or foreign value added, that is excluded from the value added estimate. The reverse situation might also be observed: The surplus of Germany with the US increases if considered in value added terms. In some cases, imbalances observed with traditional statistics might even be inverted. This is the case for the US–Spain relationship, which switches from a deficit to a small surplus with the value added measurement.

The new approach redistributes an economy's total gross trade by partner country according to the value added criteria. In that sense, the revised US trade balance highlights that the deficit with the PRC is reduced while it becomes higher with Japan and the Republic of Korea because

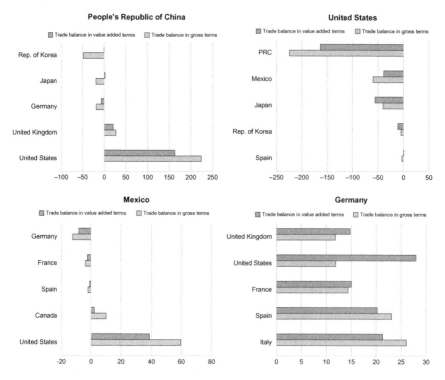

Figure 2.10. Selected bilateral trade balances with selected partners, 2008 ($ billion).

Note: PRC = People's Republic of China.

Source: World Trade Organization estimates based on Organisation for Economic Co-operation and Development inter-country input–output table.

the PRC's exports contain parts and components originated from those economies that play significant roles in East Asia's supply chains. It is worth noting that a country's total trade balance with the world (all partners) will be the same whatever the metric used (gross or value added valuation).

2.4.3. *Trade in value added and employment*

The impact of trade on employment is a core issue for policy makers. Are economies losing or winning jobs through the occurrence of global value chains? What is the net impact? These questions are difficult to answer as both demand and labor productivity play a role in the companies' decision to create, relocate, or reduce the number of jobs. For example, the loss of unskilled workers may largely stem from productivity gains. Table 2.3

Table 2.3. Average annual growth rates of employment and labor productivity, 1995–2007 (%).

	Employment	Value added	Hours worked	Labor productivity
Electronic, electrical, and optical products				
EU(15)	−0.2	5.5	−0.4	5.9
Japan	−0.1	10.6	−0.3	11.0
United States	−0.8	11.3	−0.6	11.9
Financial and insurance activities				
EU(15)	2.1	4.7	1.7	2.9
Japan	0.8	4.5	0.6	4.1
United States	1.9	3.7	2.0	1.7

Note: EU = European Union.
Source: World Trade Organization (2012).

compares two sectors, namely "electronic, electrical, and optical products" and "financial and insurance activities." The latter shows an increase in employment, while the former indicates a decrease. However, both sectors show very high productivity gains.

Another important consideration for job creation/loss comes to the forefront when measuring trade in value added terms. The Swedish National Board of Trade in 2012 developed a group of case studies on the shoe industry to examine the relevancy of anti-dumping measures. One of the cases relates to European Union (EU) imports of shoes from the PRC and highlights that when considering the entire production process, not only exports but also imports may involve domestic employment. Traditional statistics (in gross terms) lead to consideration of job losses for the EU (transferred to the PRC) only, since the entire commercial value of the shoes is only attributed to the PRC. In value added terms, while labor-intensive tasks such as manufacturing and assembly have been relocated to the PRC, the EU carried out research, design, and marketing activities, which represent a significant share in the shoes' value added. Thus, EU shoe imports from the PRC can contain value added from the EU along with related jobs, mainly in the tertiary sector.

2.4.4. *Trade in value added and international competitiveness*

The international fragmentation of production and related trade patterns lead to reconsideration of the way economies benefit from trade. Trade in value added data may lead to revisions in the interpretation of some standard macroeconomic indicators.

2.4.4.1. *Importing to export: A key point for export competitiveness*

Figure 2.11 plots the change in the vertical specialization index, or the share of foreign content in exports from 1995 to 2007 against the export performance of an economy in the manufacturing sector during the same time span. Generally speaking, a historical increase in the vertical specialization rate outlines a closer integration of an economy in GVCs. At the same time, it also indicates dependency *vis-à-vis* its production partners (see Section 2.4.5). The graph shows a positive correlation between vertical specialization and an increase in gross exports, meaning that higher integration of an economy in supply chains is related to increased export performance. In other words, economies import more and

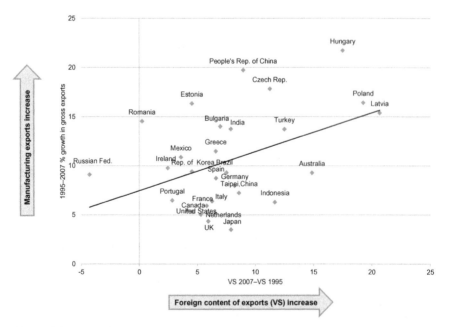

Figure 2.11. Evolution of the vertical specialization index against export performance in the manufacturing sector, 1995–2007 (%).

Source: World Trade Organization estimates based on world input–output database data.

more competitive intermediate inputs for the production of their exports. Interestingly, some recent EU members such as the Czech Republic, Hungary, Latvia, and Poland are located at the top right corner of the graph, which means that they experienced the highest rises in both vertical specialization and manufacturing exports between 1995 and 2007. This may be due to the fact that enterprises from Central and Eastern Europe, and notably SMEs, have exploited some advantages in terms of labor cost and skills to offer their services within the European production networks. This is particularly true in the IT sector, with the example of the production of Hewlett-Packard desktop computers taking place in the Czech Republic.

2.4.4.2. *Ratio of exports to GDP in value added: An idea of the actual impact of trade on an economy*

A convenient way to evaluate the importance of international trade in an economy is to calculate the share of gross exports in GDP. However, this could be a misleading indicator of export dependence as gross exports do not make the distinction between national or imported inputs used to produce the exported goods. They incorporate all the inputs, whatever their origin, in the reported values and inflate this "trade openness" ratio. Theoretically, the value added approach provides more significant ratios of exports on GDP as both trade and GDP are appreciated in the same terms.

Broadly speaking, the share of value added exports in GDP is smaller than with the gross valuation because value added exports exclude foreign value added (or imported inputs) comprised in gross export figures. On average, the exports/GDP ratio decreases by 29% with the value added approach.

Many factors can influence this ratio, such as trade policy, economic structure, and demography. However, the weight of international trade tends to be more prominent for small economies whereas larger ones may rely more on domestic demand. In that sense, plotting the value added ratio against the gross ratio on GDP (Figure 2.12) highlights that large economies tend to be on the bottom left (low ratio) and small economies on the top right corner of the graph (high ratio). With two notable exceptions, the PRC and Germany, which are at the same time major economies and top world exporters.

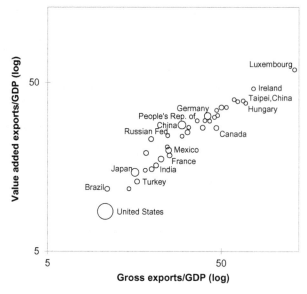

Figure 2.12. Relationship between ratios of gross and value added exports to gross domestic product, 2007.

Note: GDP = Gross domestic product.

Source: World Trade Organization estimates.

2.4.4.3. *Effective protection rates: International competitiveness of domestic value added*

Going beyond measuring nominal protection on goods, mainly computed using customs tariffs, the effective protection rate (EPR) allows quantifying the additional value added a domestic firm collects by operating within the customs territory, compared to what it could obtain if international prices were prevalent (zero tariff situation).[15] This indicator combines both market access data (tariffs) and input–output matrices and estimates the level of actual protection afforded by import duties to national producers involved in supply chains. EPRs are therefore an indicator of the anti-export bias created by the tariff structure, as domestic industries benefiting from high EPR have no incentive to operate in the international market. As mentioned by Diakantoni and Escaith (2012), EPRs are particularly

---

[15]See Diakantoni and Escaith (2012).

relevant when analyzing tariff schedules from a trade in value added perspective.

The effective protection rate formula for a sector j can be expressed as the difference between the nominal protection applied to the sector minus the average tariff paid on the required inputs from all supplying sectors i

$$\text{EPR}_j = \frac{t_j - \left(\sum_i t_i \cdot a_{ij}\right)}{1 - \sum_i a_{ij}},$$

where a_{ij} are coefficients calculated from the input–output matrix representing the shares of the inputs (domestic and imported) in the final output, t_j is the nominal protection on sector j and t_i is the nominal protection on inputs purchased from sector i. The calculation of effective protection rates is a two-step calculation and requires computation of nominal rates of protection.

The concept of EPR can be illustrated with a simple example of production of a garment which necessitates textile as an input. If the country of production imposes a 20% tariff on imported garments (the finished good), but no tariff on textiles (the raw material), the value added from the domestic garment producer benefits from a higher effective rate of protection per dollar of value added than if textiles were also subject to a tariff. Thus, if tariffs on inputs (raw materials or semi-finished goods) go down more rapidly than tariffs on finished goods, effective protection may rise even when average tariffs go down. On the contrary, if the total value of the tariffs on importable inputs exceeds that applied to finished goods, the effective rate of protection decreases and can even be negative. Negative effective protection ends up in a net loss for producers and discriminates them against imported goods.

Figure 2.13 shows the evolution of nominal and EPRs of manufactures, for some Asian developing economies in 1995 and 2005. Manufactures' EPRs were positive for all economies. Most EPRs declined between 1995 and 2005, mainly reflecting the effects of multilateral negotiations and the downward trend of applied tariffs, without omitting the accessions of the PRC and Taipei,China to the WTO. On the contrary, Malaysia and the Republic of Korea faced an increase in their EPRs during the same period. This might be related to exchange rate effects, increases

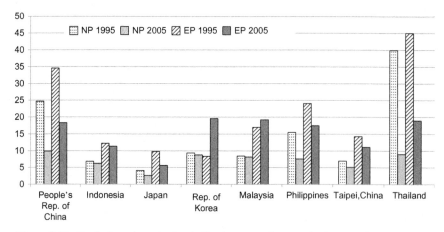

Figure 2.13. Evolution of nominal and effective protection rates in the manufacturing sector in selected Asian economies, 1995 and 2005 (%).

Note: EP = Effective protection, NP = Nominal protection.

Source: Diakantoni and Escaith (2012).

in nominal protection rates of some manufacturing sectors, and/or tariff escalation structures persisting in the tariff schedules. An increase in the EPRs is perceived from domestic producers as an incentive to supply goods domestically.

By definition, nominal and effective protection are interlinked and should be interpreted together. Increasing nominal protection will increase effective protection and will induce producers to supply goods domestically even if domestic costs are higher than exporting to international markets. On the other hand, nominal protection in the domestic market does not provide any benefit to domestic producers that export their goods. Moreover, protection of goods used as inputs in the production chain will raise the production costs and provide negative effective protection to exports. To eliminate protection in intermediate inputs, some economies have created EPZs, where imported inputs are available for domestic producers duty free.

2.4.5. *Consequences and risks associated with the interdependency of economies*

The organization of GVCs relies on each country or company's comparative advantage in specific tasks (see Section 2.5). This has led to international fragmentation of production and resulted in interdependency among economies. An examination of current industrial and trade patterns provides some evidence of such a geographical interconnectedness.

As shown before, competitiveness of countries and their export performance increasingly depends on imported inputs. When a country exports an input for further processing and re-imports it as part of another product, the imported good contains value added from the country itself. This is sometimes referred to as "circular trade." For example, the case study from the Swedish National Board of Trade (2012) demonstrated that a pair of shoes imported by the EU from the PRC could include more than 50% of value added that originated in the EU, since research, design, and marketing services activities, which largely contribute to the shoes' value, take place in Europe.

Since the country of origin is blurred (see Section 2.5), policy makers should be aware that so called "national products" may be produced outside the nation. On the contrary, products of foreign trademarks may be manufactured in the domestic market. For instance, the French car manufacturer Dacia (Renault group) produces the Logan model in Morocco for export to the French and Spanish markets.

As a consequence of such interdependency between economies, protectionist measures such as tariffs increase, countervailing, anti-dumping measures,[16] or "buy national" engagement may have counterproductive effects on the economies and enterprises they are supposed to protect. Knowing that GVCs are very sensitive to variations in transaction costs, national companies may not be competitive enough to take part in GVCs further to the application of trade protection measures. When intermediate products and related value added crisscross the planet in producing final products, tariff increases or anti-dumping measures may involve side effects in that "taxing your imports means taxing your exports." This is especially the case for companies involved in re-export activities which, by definition, rely on imported goods. The profit margin per unit of product is low in such cases, thus making them vulnerable to tariff increases (even minor ones). The functioning or competitiveness of the

---

[16]Anti-dumping duties apply to products sold at or below the price in the home country while countervailing duties are used to offset the benefits of subsidies granted to the exporting industries. The rules of origin are a determining factor in judging and levying such duties or offsets.

entire production structure may also be jeopardized by technical constraints applied to one link (country or enterprise) of the international chain. Moreover, fluctuating changes in trade policy will increase uncertainty and limit the inclination of both domestic and foreign investors to enter into long-term agreements.

The value added trade approach gives indications on the degree of integration and related dependency of an economy on GVCs as well as on trade flows exchanged with its network partners. Accounting for foreign value added content in a nation's exports can lead to greater awareness of mutual dependency. The level of domestic value added that returns as imports can also be estimated and provides a clear incentive against protectionist measures, notably when associating value added with employment (see Section 2.4).

Another risk linked to the interconnection of companies is the rapid propagation of macroeconomic shocks or consequences of natural disasters among countries involved in global production. Table 2.4 presents results of a simulation combining II–O table with the Ghosh model, to visualize supply-side transmission channels of a macroeconomic shock resulting from an exogenous increase in the cost of intermediate supplies. The idea was to estimate the disruptive effect of the March 2011 earthquake and tsunami in Japan. According to the table, Taipei,China, and Thailand are the economies most exposed to the supply shock, followed closely by Malaysia. Electronics manufacturers in the Philippines undergo a 7.4% increase in production costs following the natural disaster in Japan, the highest rise for this sector. All these economies are tightly embedded in regional and global supply chains and this is why they face significant increases in production costs due to a shortage of components originally imported from Japan. The PRC is less affected even if some of its industries, such as the "computers and electronic equipment" sector, show high vulnerability. The US is the least affected economy, possibly due to its large size and the capacity to produce national inputs for its industry. However, this average picture hides the fact that at the micro level, some individual firms are deeply dependent on Asian supply chains, and therefore might be more severely affected.

Table 2.4. Sectoral transmission of a supply-driven shock emanating from the Japanese industries for selected economies and sectors, 2008.

Supply shock from Japan to:[a]	People's Rep. of China	Indonesia	Rep. of Korea	Malaysia	Philippines	Taipei,China	Thailand	United States	Average (all economies)[b]
Chemical products	0.7	0.3	**2.2**	**2.1**	1.0	**3.2**	1.0	0.3	1.4
Petroleum and petro products	0.1	0.0	0.0	0.7	0.3	0.1	0.0	0.1	0.3
Rubber products	0.6	0.6	1.7	1.1	1.2	**2.6**	1.3	0.4	1.3
Non-metallic mineral products	0.5	0.4	0.8	1.3	0.7	1.2	1.2	0.2	0.9
Metals and metal products	1.0	1.4	**2.8**	**4.5**	**2.2**	**3.6**	**2.7**	0.4	**2.4**
Industrial machinery	1.4	**4.9**	**2.9**	**3.1**	**2.3**	**5.0**	**7.5**	0.6	**3.5**
Computers and electronic equipment	**3.6**	1.5	**3.0**	**4.3**	**7.4**	**5.6**	**5.7**	0.8	**3.9**
Other electrical equipment	**2.3**	1.4	**3.0**	**4.3**	1.9	**5.2**	**6.3**	0.6	**3.2**
Transport equipment	1.4	1.6	**2.9**	**3.8**	**2.1**	**3.4**	**5.8**	1.0	**2.8**
Other manufacturing products	0.9	1.0	**2.7**	**2.4**	1.2	**4.2**	1.7	0.4	1.8
Average (all sectors)[b]	1.2	1.3	**2.2**	**2.8**	**2.0**	**3.4**	**3.3**	0.5	**2.2**

Notes: [a]Percentage increase in sectoral domestic production costs resulting from a 30% raise in the price of intermediate inputs imported from Japan. Results higher than 2% are highlighted in bold.
[b]Simple average.

Source: Adapted from Escaith and Gonguet (2011), based on IDE-JETRO Asian input–output tables.

2.5. Are Traditional Rules and Principles in Question?

2.5.1. *Rules of origin*

There is surprisingly little said on trade policy recommendations for GVCs.[17] Do supply chains need different trade governance? The rationale behind trade in value added is that rules of origins are blurred in a globalized economy and for this reason it is appropriate to complement gross trade statistics with estimates on trade in value added. Indeed, conventional trade statistics attribute the entire commercial value of an imported good to the last country of the production chain, which can be biased. Products of a certain country may actually include very little value added of this last country.

Rules of origin are defined as "those laws, regulations and administrative determinations of general application by any Member to determine the country of origin of goods" (WTO 1995). They are important for imports under preferential arrangements and for the application of anti-dumping or countervailing duties, and tariff quotas. According to these rules, the origin of a product may change whenever a "substantial transformation" has been made on the good during a manufacturing step or when the product changes of name, tariff code, character, or use.

The economic reality behind the "Made in ..." label stamped on goods has become complex and can be illustrated by the example of the Boeing 787 Dreamliner. Figure 2.14 presents the various geographical origins of the parts and components used to construct the airplane. According to rules

Boeing relies on foreign suppliers to produce about 70% of the Dreamliner:

United States	Italy	Japan	Australia	Republic of Korea	People's Republic of China	Sweden	France	United Kingdom	Canada

Figure 2.14. The Boeing 787 Dreamliner: Geographical fragmentation of production. *Source*: Based on Graphic News infographic.

---

[17]See Swedish National Board of Trade (2012), p. 11.

of origin as well as in traditional export statistics, the US will be defined as the "country of origin" of this airplane, although only 30% of its components are national ones. Generally speaking, attributing the entire value of an imported good to the last country of a production chain may be biased. In many cases, especially for manufactured products, we do not deal with products entirely "Made in" a specific country, but rather "Made in the World."

2.5.2. *The notion of comparative advantage*

The economic literature uses revealed comparative advantage (RCA) as an indicator to judge an economy's performance for specific products. In its simplest form, RCA is defined as the share of a sector in a country's total exports as compared to the world average of the same sector in world exports. This indicator is often used as a synthetic measure of international competitiveness. However, the relevancy of RCA, like for other traditional "market share" indicators, should be re-evaluated in a globalized world. The trade in value added approach provides an interesting complement for the measure of comparative advantage since it excludes double counting of intermediate inputs unlike traditional statistics. This way, economies positioned in the downstream part of the supply chain will not present overstated comparative advantages by incorporating the value added from upstream partners. Generally speaking, the value added estimate enables identification of new comparative advantages, notably in the area of services (see Section 2.4).

Figure 2.15 is a 45° plot that compares the traditional and the value added measure of RCA in the machinery and transport equipment sector for certain economies. As a general rule, when the indicator is larger (smaller) than 1, the economy is supposed to have a trade comparative advantage (disadvantage) with regard to other economies in the sector. Furthermore, economies above the 45° line are more competitive in value added terms. This is especially the case for few East Asian economies such as Japan, the Republic of Korea, and Taipei,China that present a high value added RCA due perhaps to their role as components and services providers within Asian supply chains. On the other hand, the PRC and Mexico face a reduced RCA in value added terms, which reflects the low level of domestic value added involved in processing trade in which both countries are heavily engaged.

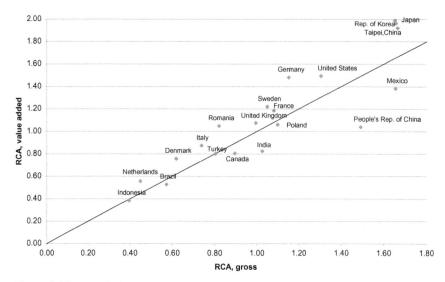

Figure 2.15. Revealed comparative advantage in gross and value added terms in selected economies, machinery, and transport equipment, 2007.

Note: RCA = Revealed comparative advantage.

Source: World Trade Organization estimates.

However, this calculation of RCA, be it in gross or value added terms, may raise additional issues. Indeed, the RCA indicator relies on product- or sector-based classifications and may not reflect properly the reality of GVCs that are organized at the task level. Nowadays, comparative advantages between economies or companies lie more in carrying out specific activities than in producing final products. As for the Apple iPhone example, traditional trade statistics show a comparative advantage for the PRC in iPhones, that is in the technology-intensive area. A decomposition of the geographical origins of the iPhone components,[18] which to some extent reflects countries' value added contribution, reveals, however, that the PRC's comparative advantage is in labor-intensive assembling tasks. As an illustration of this, the label at the back of the iPhone is now "Assembled in China" and not "Made in China."

This raises numerous questions: How should indicators, especially RCA, be compiled at the task level? What are the tasks to be considered, and

[18] See Xing and Detert (2010).

how are they to be defined? The conceptualization of industrial tasks within the existing statistical frameworks might bring up some issues, especially for trade in services statistics that are based on balance of payments, and do not have the required detail of information. Such types of questions should be addressed in the future in order to collect and compile adequate data for the analysis of GVCs. Some international organizations and institutions have already tackled these issues and developed methodologies and tools. Eurostat, for example, has established a survey on the international sourcing of companies relying on a classification of business functions that makes the distinction between core and support activities.

2.6.   Some Trade Policy Incentives and Directions to Promote GVCs

In 2012–2013, the WTO conducted a joint survey with the OECD, in cooperation with other organizations, on monitoring and evaluation of Aid-for-Trade (AfT) activity. This exercise enabled the highlighting and confirmation of the main obstacles faced by developing and least-developed countries to integrate into GVCs and develop their trade.

Effective GVCs need to monitor and optimize transaction costs throughout the entire production process. Indeed, excessive costs appearing in any country can rapidly jeopardize the entire chain. This is why reduction of tariffs applied to intermediate goods and inputs exchanged within GVCs is advocated, as it leads to productivity gains and better export competitiveness. As an example, Canada experimented with large cuts in tariffs on input goods, with good results in the industries that benefited from them.

Cost-effective infrastructure services, such as logistics, transport, shipping, and communication technologies, which are intensively used across GVCs, were also cited by the OECD–WTO AfT survey respondents as crucial to enter and move up the value chain. Performing infrastructure attracts investment and fosters the development of supply chains. Such services are also cost-effective as they are shared by numerous companies and partner countries.

The role of trade facilitation, which has been a core topic of negotiation at the WTO since the Singapore Ministerial Conference (1996), is all the more important when production is fragmented between countries. Cost and time to trade at the border is a classical feature of trade facilitation.

The efficiency and simplification of customs procedures are decisive for economies to integrate into supply chains. Therefore, relevant trade policies may focus on the automation and modernization of customs administrative operations that have a huge impact on firms' competitiveness.

Generally speaking, setting up business-friendly trade policies with a favorable environment, such as tax incentives, good infrastructure, or specialized workforce, is of high importance for the expansion of supply chains and for developing countries to join the global production.

2.7. Conclusion

Global value chains require an analytical tool that complements the analysis of trade flows with respect to a number of economic questions. The estimates of trade flows in value added terms reveal a number of preliminary messages about the present economic environment. Services are much more important than conventional trade statistics make out. Also, international competitiveness depends on imports when considering the production. This impacts a number of trade indicators such as the trade-to-GDP ratio, bilateral trade balances, and revealed comparative advantage. International input–output tables facilitate the calculation of a number of indicators such as the effective protection rate. While trade measured in value added terms may affect certain indicators, questions can be raised to which extent this approach may influence trade governance. Thus, some procedures established within the multilateral trading system, such as rules of origin or trade remedies measures (such as anti-dumping), may impact a country's own producers and exporters.

References

Burrows, P. 1995. Texas Instruments' Global Chip Payoff. *Business Week*, 7 August.

Daudin, G., C. Rifflart, and D. Schweisguth. 2011. Who Produces for Whom in the World Economy? *Canadian Journal of Economics* 44(4): 1409–1538.

Diakantoni, A. and H. Escaith. 2012. Reassessing Effective Protection Rates in a Trade in Tasks Perspective: Evolution of Trade Policy in "Factory Asia." WTO Staff Working Paper ERSD-2012-13.

Escaith, H. and F. Gonguet. 2011. International Supply Chains as Real Transmission Channels of Financial Shocks. *Journal of Financial Transformation* 31(March): 83–97.

Hummels, D., J. Ishii, and K.-M. Yi. 2001. The Nature and Growth of Vertical Specialization in World Trade. *Journal of International Economics* 54(1): 75–96.

Johnson, R. and G. Noguera. 2012. Accounting for Intermediates: Production Sharing and Trade in Value Added. *Journal of International Economics* 86(2): 224–236.

Koopman, R., Z. Wang, and S.-J. Wei. 2012. Tracing Value Added and Double Counting in Gross Exports. NBER Working Paper No. 18579.

Kraemer, L., G. Linden, and J. Dedrick. 2011. Capturing Value in Global Networks: Apple's iPad and iPhone. UC Irvine and Berkeley and Syracuse University.

Linden, G., L. Kraemer, and J. Dedrick. 2007. Who Captures Value in a Global Innovation System? The Case of Apple's iPod. Irvine, CA: UC Irvine Personal Computing Industry Center.

Los, B., E. Dietzenbacher, R. Stehrer, M. Timmer, and G. De Vries. 2012. Trade Performance in Internationally Fragmented Production Networks: Concepts and Measures. WIOD Working Paper No. 11.

Sissons, A. 2011. *More Than Making Things: A New Future for Manufacturing in a Service Economy*. London: The Work Foundation.

Stehrer, R. 2012. Trade in Value Added and the Value Added of Trade. WIOD Working Paper No. 8.

Sturgeon, T. and O. Memedovic. 2011. *Mapping Global Value Chains: Intermediate Goods Trade and Structural Change in the World Economy*. Vienna: UNIDO.

Swedish National Board of Trade. 2010. Servicification of Swedish Manufacturing.

Swedish National Board of Trade. 2012. Business Reality and Trade Policy — Closing the Gap.

Tempest, R. 1996. Barbie and the World Economy. *Los Angeles Times*, 22 September.

WTO (World Trade Organization). 1995. The Results of the Uruguay Round of Multilateral Trade Negotiations — The Legal Texts.

WTO. 2012. 15 Years of the Information Technology Agreement Trade, Innovation and Global Production Networks.

WTO and IDE-JETRO (World Trade Organization and Institute of Developing Economies, Japan External Trade Organization). 2011. *Trade Patterns and Global Value Chains in East Asia: From Trade in Goods to Trade in Tasks*. Geneva: WTO.

Xing, Y. and N. Detert. 2010. How the iPhone Widens the United States Trade Deficit with the People's Republic of China. ADBI Working Paper No. 257. Tokyo: Asian Development Bank Institute.

Chapter 3

OECD Inter-Country Input–Output Model
and Policy Implications

*Norihiko Yamano**

The inter-country input–output model has regained attention from various policy areas with increased participation of countries in the global production networks. The conventional analytical framework, based on a single country database, is not sufficient to perform effective empirical analyses, since economic integration with neighboring countries have increased the magnitude of international spillover and feedback effects. This chapter discusses the statistical challenges based on the experience of developing the OECD inter-country input–output model.

3.1. Introduction

In recent years, the international division of labor and trade flows between countries have increased dramatically. This "globalization" is partially facilitated by the development of transportation and communication infra-structure as well as ongoing negotiations of regional free trade agreements. As a consequence, intermediate products used in production supply chains have become increasingly interdependent on foreign economies in both developed and developing economies. Both the Organisation for Economic Co-operation and Development (OECD) and non-OECD economies have gradually increased international imports from the mid-1990s to the end of the 2000s (Figure 3.1). These increases in international procurement are also confirmed from the input–output statistics. The share of imported goods and services in total intermediate inputs of OECD countries increased from 12.2% in the mid-1990s to 16.2% in the mid-2000s.[1]

---

*This chapter represents the views of the author and not necessarily those of the OECD.
[1]The OECD input–output database is available at http://www.oecd.org/sti/inputoutput.

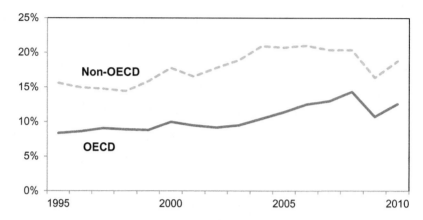

Figure 3.1. Intermediate imports-to-gross domestic product ratio.

OECD = Organisation for Economic Co-operation and Development.
Note: See Appendix 3A.1 tables for economies of OECD and non-OECD members and sector classification.
Sources: OECD/UN National Accounts, OECD BTDIxE 2013.

Other notable changes are observed in expenditure behavior of households and industry. The share of imported goods increased in the OECD countries, particularly in capital goods during the 1995–2010 period, while the import penetration ratio gradually decreased in the non-OECD economies (Figure 3.2).

Underlying this general trend of increasing reliance on foreign economies, both in terms of intermediate source and export demand market, many countries are experiencing the inevitable impact of economic fluctuations in foreign economies. In other words, employment and economic growth in each country are highly affected by demand and supply shocks caused by changes in international supply chains, global competition in final and intermediate goods, and propagation of financial systemic risks and natural disasters. In order to fully incorporate these structural changes in the final demand of domestic and foreign products, the framework of inter-industry (input–output) models can provide useful insights for policy analyses.

However, conventional national input–output models treat export and import activities as exogenous factors in a state's economy. An inter-country input–output (ICIO) system with complete worldwide economic coverage is a way to endogenize international flows of intermediate and

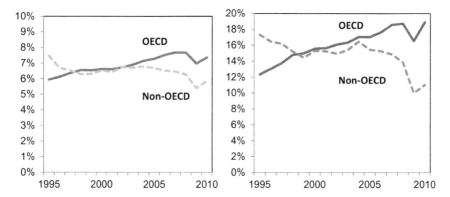

Figure 3.2. Import penetration ratio for household consumption and capital goods.

OECD = Organisation for Economic Co-operation and Development.

Note: See Appendix 3A.1 tables for economies of OECD and non-OECD members and sector classification. Personal computers and passenger car imports are equally allocated to household consumption and capital goods respectively.

Sources: OECD/UN National Accounts (final expenditures), OECD BTDIxE 2013 (imports by end-use category).

final expenditure. Building on the techniques developed and applied in multiregional input–output frameworks in the discipline of regional science, various research teams have undertaken efforts to develop ICIO models.[2]

3.2. What Does an Inter-Country Input–Output Model Represent?

The underlying data sources for an ICIO system (Figure 3.3) are national input–output or supply-use tables, national accounts series, and bilateral trade coefficients that, ideally, have been harmonized — for example, to

---

[2]Recent ICIO projects includes:

— IDE-JETRO: 9 Asian economies and United States, 1985–2005. http://www.ide.go.jp/ English/Publish/Books/Sds/material.html

— EXIOPOL: 43 countries, 2000. http://www.feem-project.net/exiopol/

— University of Sydney EORA MRIO: 187 countries, 1990–2009. http://www.worldmrio. com

— World Input–Output Database: 27 EU countries and 14 other economies, 1995–2009. http://www.wiod.org

— OECD Inter-Country Input–Output Database: 34 OECD countries, BRIICS and 18 other economies, 1995–2009. http://www.oecd.org/sti/inputoutput/.

		Country A		Country B		Country C		Final Demand			Discrepancy
		Ind. 1	Ind. 2	Ind. 1	Ind. 2	Ind. 1	Ind. 2	Country A	Country B	Country C	
Country A	Industry 1: Goods	Z_{11}^{AA}	Z_{12}^{AA}	Z_{11}^{AB}	Z_{12}^{AB}	Z_{11}^{AC}	Z_{12}^{AC}	F_1^{AA}	F_1^{AB}	F_1^{AC}	d_1^{A}
	Industry 2: Services	Z_{21}^{AA}	Z_{22}^{AA}	Z_{21}^{AB}	Z_{22}^{AB}	Z_{21}^{AC}	Z_{22}^{AC}	F_2^{AA}	F_2^{AB}	F_2^{AC}	d_2^{A}
Country B	Industry 1: Goods	Z_{11}^{BA}	Z_{12}^{BA}	Z_{11}^{BB}	Z_{12}^{BB}	Z_{11}^{BC}	Z_{12}^{BC}	F_1^{BA}	F_1^{BB}	F_1^{BC}	d_1^{B}
	Industry 2: Services	Z_{21}^{BA}	Z_{22}^{BA}	Z_{21}^{BB}	Z_{22}^{BB}	Z_{21}^{BC}	Z_{22}^{BC}	F_2^{BA}	F_2^{BB}	F_2^{BC}	d_2^{B}
Country C	Industry 1: Goods	Z_{11}^{CA}	Z_{12}^{CA}	Z_{11}^{CB}	Z_{12}^{CB}	Z_{11}^{CC}	Z_{12}^{CC}	F_1^{CA}	F_1^{CB}	F_1^{CC}	d_1^{C}
	Industry 2: Services	Z_{21}^{CA}	Z_{22}^{CA}	Z_{21}^{CB}	Z_{22}^{CB}	Z_{21}^{CC}	Z_{22}^{CC}	F_2^{CA}	F_2^{CB}	F_2^{CC}	d_2^{C}
Net taxes on products		TZ_1^{A}	TZ_2^{A}	TZ_1^{B}	TZ_2^{B}	TZ_1^{C}	TZ_2^{C}	TF^{A}	TF^{B}	TF^{C}	
Value-	Labor compensation	VL_1^{A}	VL_2^{A}	VL_1^{B}	VL_2^{B}	VL_1^{C}	VL_2^{C}				
Added	Operating surplus	VO_1^{A}	VO_2^{A}	VO_1^{B}	VO_2^{B}	VO_1^{C}	VO_2^{C}				
	Net taxes on production	VT_1^{A}	VT_2^{A}	VT_1^{B}	VT_2^{B}	VT_1^{C}	VT_2^{C}				
Output		O_1^{A}	O_2^{A}	O_1^{B}	O_2^{B}	O_1^{C}	O_2^{C}				

Figure 3.3. A simplified inter-country input–output system.

Note: Discrepancy column is adjustment for world total export and world total imports to meet the national accounts constraints.

Z_{12}^{AB}: Intermediate transaction (export) from sector 1 of country A to sector 2 of country B.

F_1^{AB}: Final demand transaction (export) from sector 1 of country A to country B.

d_1^{A}: Discrepancy of sector 1 for country A.

TZ_1^{A}: Net taxes on products of sector 1 for country A.

TF_1^{A}: Net taxes on products of final expenditure for country A.

VL_1^{A}: Labor compensation of sector 1 for country A.

VO_1^{A}: Operating surplus of sector 1 for country A.

VT_1^{A}: Net taxes on production of sector 1 for country A.

O_1^{A}: Output sector 1 for country A.

cover a common industry list. The resulting ICIO system then contains comprehensive information concerning industrial activities such as international trade, consumption, and investment by activity and sales and procurement information.

An ICIO system based on an adequate number of countries and industrial detail can therefore be useful as a data source for identifying international and sectoral transactions. It can even provide an improved alternative to publicly available bilateral gross trade figures of goods and services:

$$\text{Total exports of product } i \text{ for country } A = \sum_j Z_{ij}^{A\cdot} + F_i^{A\cdot} + d_i^{A},$$

$$\text{Total imports of product } i \text{ for country } A = \sum_j Z_{ij}^{\cdot A} + F_i^{\cdot A}.$$

Bilateral trade balance (country A's net export)

$$= \sum_i \sum_j Z_{ij}^{AB} + \sum_j F_j^{AB} - \sum_i \sum_j Z_{ij}^{BA} - \sum_j F_j^{BA}.$$

The method for constructing the OECD's ICIO database is based on the established methodology of multiregional and interregional models, with additional assumptions to meet global constraints of sectoral value-added, exports, and imports from national accounts and balance of payment. Partner shares of import and export flows of bilateral trade statistics in goods and services are also reflected as much as possible in the estimated international flows of ICIO.

Thus, the following constraints are specifically introduced at the estimation step of balancing global imports and exports:

$$EX_i^A = \sum_l \sum_i \sum_j Z_{ij}^{Al} + \sum_l \sum_i F_i^{Al},$$

$$BTD_i^{AB} EX_i^A = \left(\sum_i \sum_j Z_{ij}^{AB} + \sum_i F_i^{AB} \right),$$

where EX_i^A is exports reported in country A's national accounts statistics and BTD_i^{AB} is country B's share in country A's exports in bilateral trade statistics (total goods and services).

Data sources and intermediate analytical databases used to develop the OECD's ICIO are summarized as follows:

- Statistics submitted by national statistical institutions.
- Annual National Accounts (OECD and UN).
- Input–output and supply-use tables (national sources, Eurostat, Asian Development Bank).
- Bilateral international merchandise trade statistics (UN Comtrade and OECD ITCS).
- Bilateral trade in services (OECD, UN, and Eurostat).
- Balance of payments (national sources and IMF).
- Equivalent OECD harmonized intermediate products.
- Structural Analysis Database (STAN).
- Harmonized format input–output (I–O) database.

- Bilateral trade database by industry and by endues (BTDIxE).
- Bilateral trade in services for I–O analysis (EBTSI).
- Adjustments for ICIO development.
- Re-exports exclusion adjustments for exports and imports flows of national accounts based trade figures using I–O import matrices and merchandise trade statistics.
- System of National Accounts (SNA) benchmarked I–O and trade in goods and services.
- Estimation of update I–O tables for reference years using close year information.
- Imputed trade flows for goods and services by opposite trade flows.

3.3.   Relevant Policy Areas

As countries have become increasingly dependent on external markets, economic modeling using ICIO systems has regained attention. With its specific information on international transactions between target countries, a good ICIO database can be very useful for a range of policy analyses. In particular, environmental and trade policy analysts are supplementing their conventional approaches with information concerning international spillover and feedback effects drawn from ICIO systems.

3.3.1.   *Trade policies*

Indicators based on an ICIO system can provide both conventional and alternative viewpoints of our understanding of bilateral trade relationships, the depth of interdependency due to international supply networks, as well as new measures of comparative advantage and productivity. Most notably, since conventional bilateral trade balances based on gross measures of exports and imports can be misleading, due to the significant international flows of manufactured intermediates, an ICIO system can be used to develop measures of trade in value added terms (WTO and IDE-JETRO 2011; OECD and WTO 2013).

There are various areas where measuring trade in value added may bring a new perspective:

Global imbalances: With respect to a country's overall trade surplus or deficit with the rest of the world, measures based on gross trade flows and value-added measures are consistent. However, measures of bilateral trade based on gross concepts, can present a misleading picture of who ultimately benefits from the trade and exaggerate the importance of countries at the end of value chains. Value-added measures of bilateral trade better reflect who benefits, both in monetary terms but also, by extension, employment terms.

Market access and trade disputes: Conventional measures may create risk of protectionist responses that target countries at the end of global value chains, on the basis of inaccurate perception of the origin of trade imbalances. Indeed "beggar thy neighbor" strategies can turn out to be "beggar thyself" miscalculations.

For most economies in Asia and the Pacific, domestic value added is not necessarily created by final demands in neighboring regions (Association of Southeast Asian Nations and East Asia) (Figure 3.4). This implies that

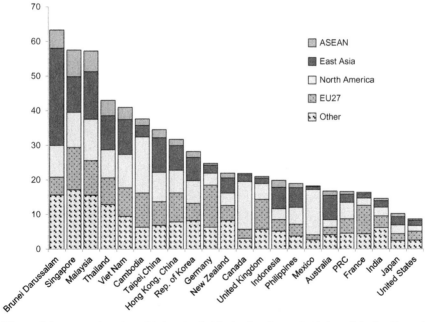

Figure 3.4. Domestic value added embodied in foreign demand. (Asia and the Pacific and selected economies, % of GDP).

Note: ASEAN = Association of Southeast Asian Nations, EU = European Union, PRC = People's Republic of China.

Source: OECD-WTO Trade in Value-Added, 2013 [FDDVA].

demand from households and industries of North American and European countries have significant impacts on Asian economies.

3.3.2. *Trade, growth, and employment*

While there are concerns that imports threaten domestic jobs, the reality is that jobs are increasingly created as part of global value chains. Trade flows in value-added terms indicate where jobs are created and highlight the benefits of trade for all economies involved in the value chain. Interdependencies within global value chains are key to explaining competitiveness of countries and productivity gains that capitalize on these dependencies. Trade in value added and jobs engaged in industrial activity by sector serve as proxy indicators for jobs embodied in international trade. For example, Figure 3.5 indicates that relatively smaller developing economies in Europe significantly rely on foreign demand.

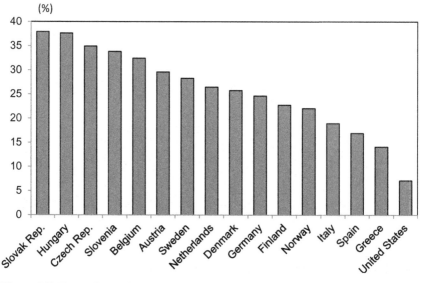

Figure 3.5. Domestic employment created by foreign final demand (% of total employment).

Sources: OECD ICIO Database, 2013; OECD STAN (employment numbers engaged).

3.3.3. Ecological footprint issues

Changes in consumption and production locations have significantly altered global patterns of consumption-based ecological impacts and production-based ecological impacts. For example, efforts to mitigate greenhouse gas (GHG) emissions, such as the Kyoto Protocol, will be less effective in reducing global emissions of GHG if countries with emission commitments relocate their carbon-intensive production activities to countries without such commitments, particularly if production in the latter countries is GHG-intensive. The ICIO and International Energy Agency's energy statistics (fuel-combustion-based CO_2 and international electricity transfer), together with other industry statistics, can be used to estimate the effects of international transfers of CO_2 emissions among economies (Figure 3.6).

Moreover, ICIOs are useful for analyzing local pollution and ecological footprints. For example, analysis of freshwater extraction, soil degradation, and biodiversity impacts have turned to ICIO models for insights (EXIOPOL[3] and Lenzen *et al.* 2012).

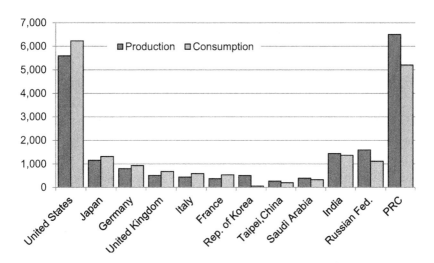

Figure 3.6. Production and consumption based CO_2 emissions, 2008 (Mt CO_2).
Source: OECD ICIO Database, 2013; IEA CO_2 emissions from fuel combustions.

---

[3] See project information at http://www.feem-project.net/exiopol/.

3.3.4. Risk management

The 2008–2009 financial crisis was characterized by a synchronized trade collapse in many economies, as the effects of a drop in demand fed through to countries located upstream in the global value chain. A better understanding of value-added trade flows would provide tools for policy makers to identify the transmission of macroeconomic shocks and adopt appropriate policy responses.

Also, more recent unexpected events such as the March 2011 earthquake in Japan and the autumn 2011 flood in Thailand raised some understandable concerns over global supply chains. The rise of global supply chains has increased the sensitivity of national economies to natural disasters and shocks in other parts of the world. ICIO models can contribute to a better understanding of direct and indirect vulnerability to unexpected events, to inform countries about possible pre-emptive actions to minimize impacts.

3.4. Methodological and Statistical Limitations

As discussed above, ICIOs provide useful numerical indicators for evidence-based policy making in various areas. However, constructing an ICIO table with maximum global coverage requires extremely data-intensive preparation procedures. The key issues are summarized as follows:

Collection and estimation of input–output tables in a harmonized format: While national tables are expected to comply with a standard (industry/ product) format within Europe, most other countries produce supply and use tables and/or input–output tables in their own established formats with varying industry and/or product detail. Also, the definition ("valuation") of output can vary across countries, for example with respect to treatment of taxes and subsidies.

Development of bilateral trade in goods and services consistent with the national accounts framework of each country: Reported bilateral merchandise exports and imports statistics compiled by customs offices are not, by definition, the same as estimates of exports and imports of goods in Balance of Payments (BoP) and SNA statistics and hence national I–O tables. National statisticians make numerous adjustments to transform merchandise trade in goods statistics to SNA/BoP concepts. For example, adjustments are made for the "cost, insurance, freight" (c.i.f.) element of reported merchandise imports of goods. However, for many countries such adjustments are carried out only for total goods, or at very aggregate levels. Thus, assumptions are required to link bilateral trade by industry or product groups to I–O tables. Also, adjustments may be required to account for the presence of re-exports or re-imports in official bilateral trade statistics as well as to deal with recorded flows of used (secondhand) and recycled products.

Estimation methodology of international trade and insurance margins and tariffs: International trade and insurance margins need to be explicitly estimated to link monetary transactions between countries. Actual international transaction costs are determined by various factors such as distances between countries, port efficiency, type of commodity, and fuel surcharge prices.

Incorporating and understanding firm heterogeneity: Statistics from customs databases in the People's Republic of China (PRC) suggest that the majority of exports from certain sectors are driven by foreign capital with many firms serving export markets only. Such (processing) firms may have very different characteristics than other firms in the same sector serving their domestic market. Accounting for such heterogeneity within certain sectors is particularly challenging when building an ICIO model.

Collection of employment statistics to measure trade in jobs and skills: International harmonized labor statistics, such as working hours, industry and occupation details, and skill contents, are not currently available and require considerable efforts to develop the employment profile vectors.

3.5. Conclusion

New indicators based on ICIO systems can support evidence-based policy making processes, particularly for areas related to productivity and competitiveness. New information on comparative advantage can help countries better understand global production networks and determine optimal strategies for taking advantage of resource efficiencies within global production chains.

The framework of ICIO systems still follows the SNA principles, so the model is basically restricted to monetary transactions between sectors of a specific reference year. Physical transactions, capital formation over years, and income transfers such as payments for royalties, dividends, and labor income dividends are not yet in the scope of ordinary ICIO models. This additional type of statistical data information integrated within an ICIO system would provide a deeper understanding of the evolution of global production networks.

Appendix 3A

Table 3A.1. OECD ICIO system target economies.

OECD				Non-OECD			
1	Australia	18	Japan	35	Argentina	52	Russian Federation
2	Austria	19	Republic of Korea	36	Brazil	53	Saudi Arabia
3	Belgium	20	Luxembourg	37	Brunei Darussalam	54	Singapore
4	Canada	21	Mexico	38	Bulgaria	55	South Africa
5	Chile	22	Netherlands	39	Cambodia	56	Thailand
6	Czech Rep.	23	New Zealand	40	PRC	57	Viet Nam
7	Denmark	24	Norway	41	Taipei,China	58	Rest of the World
8	Estonia	25	Poland	42	Cyprus		
9	Finland	26	Portugal	43	Hong Kong, China		
10	France	27	Slovak Republic	44	India		
11	Germany	28	Slovenia	45	Indonesia		
12	Greece	29	Spain	46	Latvia		
13	Hungary	30	Sweden	47	Lithuania		
14	Iceland	31	Switzerland	48	Malaysia		
15	Ireland	32	Turkey	49	Malta		
16	Israel	33	United Kingdom	50	Philippines		
17	Italy	34	United States	51	Romania		

Table 3A.2. Sector classification of OECD ICIO system.

ISIC rev3	Industry	ISIC rev3	Industry
01, 02, 05	Agriculture, hunting, forestry and fishing	20	Wood and products of wood and cork
10–14	Mining and quarrying	21–22	Pulp, paper, paper products, printing and publishing
15–16	Food products, beverages and tobacco	23	Coke, refined petroleum products and nuclear fuel
17–19	Textiles, textile products, leather and footwear	24	Chemicals

(Continued)

Table 3A.2. (*Continued*)

ISIC rev3	Industry	ISIC rev3	Industry
25	Rubber and plastics products	50–52	Wholesale and retail trade;
26	Other non-metallic mineral		repairs
	products	55	Hotels and restaurants
27	Basic metals	60–63	Transport and storage
28	Fabricated metal products	64	Post and telecommunications
29	Machinery and equipment, nec	65–67	Finance and insurance
30	Office, accounting and	70	Real estate activities
	computing machinery	71	Renting of machinery and
31	Electrical machinery and		equipment
	apparatus, nec	72	Computer and related activities
32	Radio, television and	73	Research and development
	communication equipment	74	Other business activities
33	Medical, precision and optical	75	Public administration and
	instruments		defense; compulsory social
34	Motor vehicles, trailers and		security
	semi-trailers	80	Education
35	Other transport equipment	85	Health and social work
36–37	Manufacturing nec; recycling	90–93	Other community, social and
	(include furniture)		personal services
40–41	Utility	95	Private households with
45	Construction		employed persons

References

Lenzen, M., K. Kanemoto, D. Moran, and A. Geschke. 2012. Mapping the Structure of the World Economy. *Environmental Science and Technology* 46(15): 8374–8381.

OECD and WTO (Organisation for Economic Co-operation and Development and World Trade Organization). 2013. Measuring Trade in Value Added: An OECD–WTO Joint Initiative. http://oe.cd/tiva.

WTO and IDE-JETRO (World Trade Organization and Institute of Developing Economies, Japan External Trade Organization). 2011. *Trade Patterns and Global Value Chains in East Asia: From Trade in Goods to Trade in Tasks*. Geneva: WTO.

Chapter 4

Estimating the Upper Limits of Value Added in the People's Republic of China's Processing Exports

We apply a direct approach to estimate domestic value added embedded in the People's Republic of China's (PRC) processing exports. The estimates suggest that the domestic value added of processing exports and processing high-tech exports gradually increased from 30% and 25% to 44% and 45%, respectively, between 1997 and 2012. On the other hand, the domestic content of processing exports with supplied materials fell to 14% from its peak at 35%. In 2012, the domestic value added of the PRC's total exports remained below 77%. Compared to our estimates, OECD's TiVA database significantly overestimates the domestic content of the PRC's exports. TiVA's estimates are also inconsistent with the fact that the share of processing exports in the PRC's total exports has decreased steadily. In addition, we show that the PRC's processing exports demonstrate significant heterogeneity across its trading partners; processing exports account for a large portion of total exports to high-income countries but a relatively small portion of exports to low-income countries.

4.1. Introduction

The proliferation of global value chains (GVCs) has fundamentally challenged economic implications of conventional trade statistics, recorded with gross values of cross-border goods flows. In open macroeconomic models, imports of a country are generally assumed to represent domestic demand for foreign goods and services. However, in supply chain trade, a substantial part of a country's imports have nothing to do with domestic demand, but are induced by the demand of the destination market located at the end of the GVC. Taking the People's Republic of China (PRC), the global assembly center of manufacturing products, as an example, it imported US$480 billion, about 26% of its total imports in 2012, neither for domestic consumption nor for investment, but for manufacturing products serving foreign demand. Empirical studies usually apply gross exports to measure export capacity of an economy and assume the technology embedded in the exports represent the technology capacity of the exporting countries. In supply chain trade, many countries involved in GVCs need to import parts and components as intermediate inputs. As a result, gross values of exports consist of a significant portion of value added generated by foreign countries, and thus greatly exaggerate actual export capacities, in particular of countries specializing in assembly and other labor-intensive tasks. Similarly, each individual country along GVCs performs only limited tasks required for finished products. Overall technology achievement embedded in finished products represents the combination of technology capacities of all countries participating in supply chains. It is thus misleading to utilize finished products as a proxy of technology advancement for a country that performs limited tasks in the production of finished products. The iPhone is a typical example. All iPhones sold in the global market are exclusively assembled in and exported from the PRC. However, using the iPhone as a proxy to gauge the PRC's technology capability and competitiveness in smartphones would be misleading, as workers of the PRC simply assemble imported parts together and contribute only 3.6% of the total value added of a ready-to-use iPhone (Xing and Detert 2010).

To a large extent, the rapid expansion of GVCs has facilitated rising trade volumes worldwide. Technology progresses in production fragmentation, advancement in logistics, and liberalization in trade and foreign direct investment have enabled multinational enterprises (MNEs) to slice production processes and optimally allocate various tasks in different geographic locations. Technology innovations and cross-country production fragmentation of leading MNEs have constantly induced and amplified trade flows. However, the methodology of computing trade flows remains the same, and there has been little reform in trade statistics incorporating fundamental changes brought by the proliferation of GVCs. With the outdated trade statistics, many economic analyses on trade balances, dynamic changes of export structures, revealed comparative advantages, and so on reach conclusions inconsistent with the reality.

For instance, Rodrik (2006) argues that the sophistication of the PRC's exports far exceeded that defined by its income level. Merri (2009) claims the PRC surpassed the United States (US), European Union (EU-27), and Japan and emerged as the largest high-tech exporting country, and Scott (2012) estimates the US trade with the PRC between 2001 and 2010 eliminated 1.9 million jobs in manufacturing. These studies ignore the fact that the PRC is just a part of the GVC of the underlying products, mistakenly assuming that everything shipped out of the PRC is completely manufactured in the country.

To improve our understanding of the contribution of supply chain trade to economic development as well as to bilateral trade relations and technology innovations, it is essential to accurately measure the contribution of each country in the value chain. Hummels *et al.* (2001) use input–output tables to estimate the import content of exports, defined as vertical specialization. They find that the ratios of import contents accounted for more than 20% of exports in the underlining countries. The research emphasizes the level of specialization rather than new measures of trade flows. Koopman *et al.* (2009) argue that import contents are higher if processing exports are pervasive. They divide the PRC's exports into normal and processing exports and find that the import contents of the PRC's processing exports exceed 50%.

Global imbalances were argued to be a major factor causing the 2008 global financial crisis. At the center of debates on global imbalances is the imbalance between the PRC and the US. Many economists prescribed a significant appreciation of the yuan as an effective policy option to mitigate the imbalance and prevent similar crises in the future. Xing and Detert (2010) use the iconic iPhone as a case and argue that existing trade statistics create a distorted trade pattern and significantly exaggerate the PRC's export volumes as well as its trade surplus with the US. The Sino–US trade deficit is not a simple bilateral issue but to a large extent a multilateral one. The surge in the iPhone exports to the US from the PRC and the corresponding trade imbalance has nothing to do with the PRC's technology advancement or improvement in comparative advantages. The study illustrates unambiguously the inconsistency of conventional trade statistics with supply chain trade and provides persuasive arguments for reforming conventional trade statistics.

The findings of Xing and Detert (2010) were extensively reported and analyzed by mainstream media such as the *Wall Street Journal* and the *Financial Times*. The involvement of the global mainstream media in the debates on pitfalls of conventional trade statistics has given rise to a momentum for creating value added trade statistics. The Institute of Developing Economies, Japan External Trade Organization (IDE-JETRO 2012) first employed Asian input–output tables covering nine Asian countries as well as the US to calculate domestic and foreign contents in exports. The study suggests that in 2005 the PRC's trade deficit would be cut by half if the value added approach is adopted. In January, 2013, the Organisation for Economic Co-operation and Development (OECD) and the World Trade Organization (WTO) jointly launched the preliminary database of trade in value added (TiVA), covering 40 countries with a breakdown into 18 sectors (OECD and WTO 2013). In the race to reevaluate global trade in value added, the United Nations Conference on Trade and Development (UNCTAD 2013) also published estimates of trade in value added and analyzed the nexus between GVC participation and economic development. The report suggests that GVC participation facilitates job creation, knowledge transfer, and economic growth. Koopman *et al.* (2012) provide a rigorous theoretical framework to compute trade in value added with input–output tables. In particular, they show a way to decompose the double-counting component — that is, imports embedded with domestic value added.

Theoretically, input–output tables are a powerful tool for mapping directions and origins of trade in value added among trading nations. However, the results of input–output tables are estimates derived with strong assumptions. As a matter of fact, the estimation of value added in trade with input–output tables relies on estimates of input–output coefficients, which requires detailed estimates of the cross-country distribution of imported contents, and assumes that consumers of all economies have same preferences and consumption bundles. Conventional trade data, despite failing to outline actual distribution of value added among trading nations, are highly accurate and reliable in terms of measuring quantities of goods crossing borders. How reliable are the estimates of trade in value added with input–output tables? If the estimates of trade in value added carry very large errors, economic analysis based on the estimates will lead to similar mistakes. It is essential to scrutinize the reliability and accuracy of the estimates derived from input–output tables before we conduct rigorous econometric analysis.

In this chapter, we introduce a new method, which is independent of input–output tables, to estimate the domestic content of exports. This method depends on the availability of the statistics on aggregate imports used for producing exports. Due to the limitation of trade data, this approach may not accurately measure domestic contents embedded in exports. However, it does provide an upper limit of domestic content and can be used as a benchmark to examine the accuracy and reliability of the estimates derived from input–output tables.

Processing trade makes up about 40% of the PRC's trade and the PRC's customs authorities regularly publish statistics on processing trade in some categories. We apply this approach to the processing exports of the PRC and compare our results with those of the OECD TiVA database. The comparison suggests that the OECD TiVA substantially overestimates the domestic content of PRC exports. The TiVA estimation is also inconsistent with the fact that the share of processing exports has gradually declined.

Moreover, an investigation of the importance of processing exports in the PRC's exports to its major trading partners reveals significant heterogeneity. Processing exports account for more than 60% of the PRC's gross exports to a few industrialized countries, such as the US and Japan, while it accounts for less than 20% to some developing countries. In general, processing exports contain a large portion of foreign value added compared to normal exports. This heterogeneity of processing exports implies the domestic content of the PRC's exports varies substantially by trading partner. Generally countries along GVCs perform different tasks according to their comparative advantages. The domestic value added of a country's exports varies according to relative positions of its trading partners in the supply chain. Moreover, the domestic value added of exports to trading partners located in the same value chains may be different to that of nations not involved in the supply chains. Assuming homothetic consumer preferences and consumption bundles among trading economies in estimating trade in value added ignores this vital feature of GVCs.

The rest of the chapter is organized as follows: In the next section, we introduce our approach. In Section 4.3, we apply the method to the

PRC's data. In Section 4.4, we examine the heterogeneity of the PRC's processing exports over its major trading partners. Then, we compare our estimates with those of the OECD TiVA in Section 4.5. Section 4.6 finally summarizes the major findings.

4.2.   Estimating the Value Added in Trade: A Simple Approach

Many countries grant tariff-free status to imports used for producing exports and provide special tax incentives to firms exporting products manufactured with imported materials. To enjoy these benefits, firms importing intermediate inputs are required to declare the purposes of their imports and whether their exports are made with imported intermediate materials. In these countries, aggregated data on imports by purposes and exports with or without imported contents are available. PRC Customs collects and publishes the data of processing imports and with these data, we are able to estimate the domestic value added of exports as:

$$VA = \frac{EX - PIM}{EX} 100\%, \qquad (4.1)$$

where VA denotes the share of domestic value added in exports, EX is gross exports, and PIM is gross imports employed for producing exports. Equation (4.1) is a simple and straightforward way to compute domestic value added in exports. The accuracy of the estimates depends on data availability. In supply chain trade, exports often contain foreign value added while imports may include domestic value added, a so-called double counting issue. The mixture of domestic and foreign contents in exports and imports complicates the computation of domestic value added. However, if we trace the movement of goods across borders, it is not difficult to understand that the difference between total exports and total imports used to produce the exports should be equal to the domestic value added. Intuitively, any foreign intermediate good is first added to total imports. When final products are exported, the entire value, including the foreign content, is counted as a part of exports. Therefore, taking the differences of the two aggregates will automatically cancel out foreign value added included in both aggregated imports and exports. Similarly, in the case of domestic goods which are exported then imported back for further processing, the same value is recorded in both total exports and imports.

If it is eventually shipped abroad as final goods, its domestic value will be captured by the differences and there is no double counting issue. We will prove this intuitive explanation mathematically below.

Proposition: If EX is the aggregated gross exports of a country and PIM is the aggregated gross imports used for producing exports EX, the domestic value added of EX is equal to $(EX - PIM)$, regardless of whether PIM contains foreign value added or not.

Proof: Assume that a country exports N different final goods: E^1, $E^2, \ldots E^n$. Good E^1 becomes final consumption in the first round of being exported; good E^2 is exported in the first round, then imported back with additional foreign value added and becomes final consumption abroad after further domestic processing and being exported in round 2; good E^i becomes final consumption in round i. Before a good becomes final consumption, its domestic and foreign value added continues to increase in each round of export and import. Now, we turn to calculating the cumulative domestic value added associated with each good, then the sum of total value added of these N goods.

According to the definition, E^1 becomes final consumption abroad in the first round of being exported. Its gross export value can be defined as

$$TE_g^1 = e_1^1 + m_1^1, \tag{4.2}$$

where e_1^1 indicates domestic value added and m_1^1 foreign value added embedded in E^1. The total gross imports associated with producing good E^1 is:

$$IME_g^1 = m_1^1. \tag{4.3}$$

Subtracting (4.3) from (4.2) yields the domestic value added of good E^1:

$$TE_g^1 - IME_g^1 = e_1^1. \tag{4.4}$$

We can apply similar analysis to good E^2, which becomes final consumption abroad in the second round of exporting. In the first round, it is exported with gross value $(e_1^2 + m_1^2)$, where e_1^2 denotes domestic value added and m_1^2 is imported foreign content, then re-imported with gross import value $(e_1^2 + m_1^2 + m_2^2)$ after further processing abroad, where m_2^2 represents the new foreign value added after foreign companies process the original value $(e_1^2 + m_1^2)$. E^2 is exported as a final consumption in round 2 with incremental domestic value e_2^2, which is added after further processing at home. Hence, total gross exports associated with good E_2 is

$$TE_g^2 = \left(e_1^2 + m_1^2\right) + \left(e_1^2 + m_1^2 + e_2^2 + m_2^2\right) \tag{4.5}$$

and the total gross imports used for producing final E^2 is

$$IME_g^2 = \left(m_1^2\right) + \left(e_1^2 + m_1^2 + m_2^2\right). \tag{4.6}$$

Using Equations (4.5) and (4.6), we can derive total cumulative domestic value added of good E^2 as

$$TE_g^2 - IME_g^2 = \left(e_1^2 + e_2^2\right). \tag{4.7}$$

Following the same fashion, it is straightforward to define total gross exports due to producing final good E^n as

$$\begin{aligned}
TE_g^n &= \left(e_1^n + m_1^n\right) + \left(e_1^n + m_1^n + e_2^n + m_2^n\right) + \cdots \\
&\quad + \left(e_1^n + m_1^n + e_2^n + m_2^n + \cdots e_n^n + m_n^n\right) \\
&= \sum_{k=1}^{n} \sum_{i=1}^{k} \left(e_i^n + m_i^n\right)
\end{aligned} \tag{4.8}$$

Similarly, total imports for producing E^n can be written as

$$\begin{aligned}
IME_g^n &= \left(m_1^n\right) + \left(e_1^n + m_1^n + m_2^n\right) + \left(e_1^n + e_2^n + m_1^n + m_2^n + m_3^n\right) \\
&\quad + \cdots + \left(e_1^n + \cdots + e_{n-1}^n + m_1^n + \cdots + m_n^n\right) \\
&= \sum_{k=1}^{n} \sum_{i=1}^{k} \left(e_{i-1}^n + m_i^n\right),
\end{aligned} \tag{4.9}$$

where $e_o^n = 0$.

Subtracting (4.9) from (4.8) yields cumulative domestic value added of good E^n

$$TE_g^n - IME_g^n = \sum_{i=1}^{n} e_i^n. \tag{4.10}$$

Therefore, the aggregated gross exports of the country exporting final goods $E^1, E^2, \ldots, E^n$ can be defined as

$$EX_g = \sum_{i=1}^{n} TE_g^i, \tag{4.11}$$

and the aggregated gross imports used for producing these exports can be defined as:

$$IM_g = \sum_{i=1}^{n} IME^i. \tag{4.12}$$

Subtracting (4.12) from (4.11), we derive total domestic value added of final exports as

$$EX_g - IM_g = \sum_{k=1}^{n} \sum_{i=1}^{k} e_i^k. \tag{4.13}$$

Equation (4.13) implies that the difference of aggregated exports and aggregated imports used for producing exports is equal to the sum of total domestic value added accumulated in the whole process of producing and finally exporting goods $E^1, E^2, \ldots, E^n$.

We assume that E^i are final consumption goods and m_i^j include only foreign value added. It is possible that after E^j is exported and processed abroad with added value α, $(E^j + \alpha)$ is used as an input of E^k. In this case, the total gross exports due to producing E^k would be

$$T\hat{E}_g^k = \sum_{p=1}^{k} \sum_{i=1}^{p} \left(e_i^k + m_i^k \right) + \beta(E^j + \alpha), \tag{4.14}$$

and the total imports due to producing E^k would be

$$IM\hat{E}_g^k = \sum_{p=1}^{k} \sum_{i=1}^{p} \left(e_{i-1}^k + m_i^k \right) + \beta(E^j + \alpha), \tag{4.15}$$

where $\beta = (k - l + 1)$, assuming that in round l that $(E^j + \alpha)$ is imported as an input for producing E^k

$$T\hat{E}_g^k - IM\hat{E}_g^k = \sum_{i=1}^{k} e_i^k, \tag{4.16}$$

which is the total cumulative value added in the process of manufacturing good E^k. It is the same as equation (4.13). Hence, adding inputs from other domestically produced goods does not change the results of the calculation.

4.3. Estimating Domestic Value Added of the People's Republic of China's Processing Exports

We apply Equation (4.1) to estimate the domestic value added of the PRC's processing exports in the following categories: (i) total processing exports, (ii) processing exports with imported materials, (iii) processing exports with supplied materials, and (iv) processing high-tech exports. The PRC's customs statistics classify trade into ordinary and processing trade. Processing imports are defined as goods that are brought into the PRC to be used as intermediate goods in the manufacture of final products. Processing imports are duty free, and neither imported inputs nor finished goods produced using processing imports enter the PRC's domestic market. The processed final goods are subsequently re-exported from the PRC and are classified as processing exports. There are two kinds of processing exports: processing exports with supplied materials and processing exports made from imported materials. In the former case, firms in the PRC receive parts and components from foreign firms for further processing but do not provide financial payment to the foreign suppliers. They receive processing fees after delivering processed products to the foreign suppliers. At the beginning of the PRC's opening, because of the shortage of foreign exchange reverses, many firms signed cooperation agreements with foreign firms to engage in simple assembly with supplied materials. In the latter, domestic firms purchase intermediate materials from abroad and then export products made with imported materials either to original material suppliers or third parties.

Producing exports requires energy, which may be produced with imported oil, natural gas, and/or coal. Imported raw materials such as coppers and iron ore may also be used in the production of exports. These kinds of inputs are generally not included in processing import statistics. If we use the published processing import statistics to calculate domestic contents, equation (4.1) should be revised as

$$\text{Value Added} = \frac{EX - PIM - \alpha}{EX} \leq \frac{EX - PIM}{EX},$$

where α represents imported intermediate inputs which are not included in processing imports. Because we are unable to estimate α, the domestic value added estimated with equation (4.1) is an approximation and should be regarded as the upper limit of actual domestic content.

In 2012, the PRC's processing exports amounted to US$860 billion, about 42% of its total exports. Processing exports with imported materials made up 88% of total processing exports. Processing imports were US$480 billion, about 27% of total imports. Processing trade has been a very important modality of exports in the PRC's international trade and contributed 100% to the trade surplus (Xing 2012). Figure 4.1 shows the estimated domestic value added of processing trade. In 1993, the domestic value added consisted of 18% of processing exports. It rose steadily and

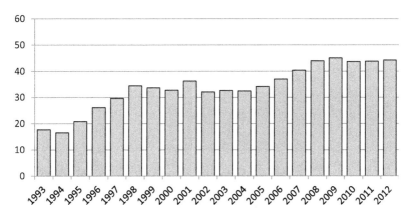

Figure 4.1. Domestic value added of processing exports from the People's Republic of China.

Source: Author's estimation using customs data from the People's Republic of China.

reached 36% by 2001, suggesting a substantial improvement in adding more domestic content. After the PRC's entry into the WTO in 2001, as more and more foreign firms relocated their assembly facilities into the country and outsourced labor-intensive tasks to firms in the PRC, the domestic value added dropped to 32% in the following year. It started to increase again in 2005 and achieved 44% by 2012, more than double the share in 1993, but remained below 50%.

In Figure 4.2, we compare the value added of two different kinds of processing exports. With regard to the definition, processing exports with supplied materials are supposed to have lower domestic content. However, before 2001, the shares of domestic value added in both categories were roughly the same. For instance, in 1995 and 1996, the shares of domestic value added of the two kinds of processing exports were at 21%. After 2000, the shares diverged and moved in opposite directions. The domestic content of processing exports with imported materials gradually increased and reached the 50% mark in 2009, while that of processing exports with supplied materials declined from its peak level of 35% to a mere 14% in 2012. Foxconn, which has a monopoly on the iPhone assembly, belongs to this category. The absolute value of processing exports with supplied

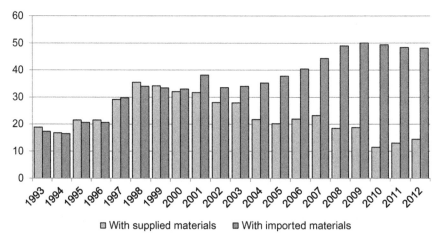

Figure 4.2. Domestic value added in two kinds of processing exports from the People's Republic of China.

Source: Author's estimation using customs data from the People's Republic of China.

materials also went down from US$116 billion to US$98 billion, implying that PRC firms have scaled down or exited from the low value added segment.

In addition, we estimate the domestic value added of processing high-tech exports. High-tech exports comprised about 31% of the PRC's manufacturing exports in 2012. In the process of economic development, the structure of exports generally evolves from resource-intensive to labor-intensive, and eventually to capital-intensive. All countries, in particular developing countries, expect to increase their share of high value added commodities and services. High value added products imply higher incomes and better jobs. The share of high-tech products is often used as a proxy to assess dynamic changes of comparative advantage and positive improvements in export structures. The PRC has emerged as the number one exporter of many information and communication technology products, such as notebook computers, digital cameras, and mobile devices. On the other hand, processing exports have been dominant in the PRC's high-tech exports. About 80% of high-tech exports were produced with imported key parts and components. To examine the actual contribution of these processed high-tech exports to technology innovations and economic development, it is essential to evaluate the domestic contents embedded in the exports. Xing (2014) estimates that the domestic value added of an iPhone assembled in the PRC is 3.6% and that of a laptop computer is 4%. The two products accounted for 15% of the PRC's total exports in 2012. These are two typical products. The overall domestic value added of the PRC's high-tech exports may be higher.

Figure 4.3 shows the estimated value added of the PRC's processing high-tech exports from 1997 to 2012. It was 27% in 1997 and gradually rose to 56% in 2001. Similar to the trend of the overall processing exports, the domestic content dropped sharply to 31% in 2002 and declined continuously to 28% in 2005, even lower than the share of overall processing exports with imported materials, which was 38%. The relatively low domestic contents questions the definition of high-tech exports under GVCs. Examining finished products, there is no doubt that smartphones, digital cameras, and notebook computers are of the high-tech category. However, the tasks performed by firms in the PRC are in the low skills category. Being involved in GVCs of high-tech products does not necessarily mean firms have

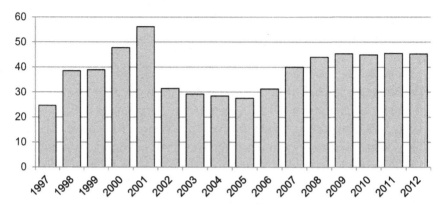

Figure 4.3. Domestic value added in high-tech exports from the People's Republic of China.

Source: Author's estimation using customs data from the People's Republic of China.

acquired key technology and skills required for manufacturing high-tech products. The domestic share of high-tech exports rose in recent years to 45%, just equal to the level of overall processing trade but remained lower than that of processing exports with imported materials.

4.4. Domestic Value Added of the People's Republic of China's Exports by Trading Partner

Homothetic preference represents one of the fundamental assumptions of the input–output approach. It assumes that, regardless of heterogeneity in resource endowments, income levels, and tasks in GVCs, all countries have identical import bundles proportional to their incomes. The assumption is problematic. First, the assumption ignores endowment and technology differences, which play a critical role in determining the task allocation among nations involved in GVCs. Second, it assumes that the composition of a country's exports to its trading partners located in the upstream of value chains is the same as trading partners in the downstream. This assumption fails to recognize special features of GVCs, where tasks are optimally allocated according to countries' comparative advantage and geographic proximity. Xing (2012) shows that the US and the EU are the major destination market of the PRC's processing exports while East Asian economies are the major source of processing imports. Hence, the domestic content of the PRC's exports with respect to the source market should be different from that to the destination market. How important is this heterogeneity? Is it trivial and can thus be ignored in estimating trade in value added?

As shown previously, the domestic value added of processing exports with imported materials is about 48%, while that of processing exports with supplied materials is much lower, about 14%. Unambiguously, the weight of processing exports affects the overall value added of exports, in particular when processing exports comprise a large portion of exports.

To examine the cross-country heterogeneity of processing exports, we calculate shares of processing exports in the PRC's top 40 destination markets in 2012. It is well known that Hong Kong, China has been functioning as a transit port for the PRC's exports to the rest of the world. We exclude Hong Kong, China in the comparison. Instead, we allocate processing exports to Hong Kong, China proportionally to the rest of the economies. Figure 4.4 presents the results. Clearly, shares of processing exports vary significantly across the trading partners. Generally, they tend to be high for developed economies, and make up 67%, 60%, and 59% of the PRC's exports to the Netherlands, Singapore, and the US, respectively. On the other hand, processing exports represent a relatively

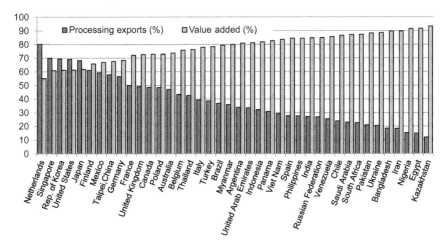

Figure 4.4. Processing exports and domestic value added of the People's Republic of China by trading partner, 2012.

Source: Author's calculations.

small portion of the exports to developing economies, for instance, about 15%, 14%, and 12% to Nigeria, Egypt, and Kazakhstan, respectively. The simple descriptive analysis implies that processing exports serve mainly industrialized economies. Applying equation (4.1), we estimate the upper limits of the domestic value added of the PRC's exports to these 40 economies. The estimates suggest that the domestic value added of the exports to the Netherlands and the US is about 62% and 67%, respectively. The upper limits of some lower-income countries, such as Egypt, Pakistan, and Kazakhstan exceed 90%. Hence, the heterogeneity of the domestic value added of the PRC's exports across destinations is too large to be ignored in the estimation of trade in value added.

4.5. Comparison of the Estimates with the Trade in Value Added Database

All published estimates of trade in value added are derived from international input–output tables. Compared with the input–output approach, the methodology adopted here is simple and straightforward. An interesting question is how reliable the estimates of this study are and whether there exists a large difference between estimates derived with the two different approaches. To answer this question, we compare our estimates with those derived from input–output tables. To do so, we first estimate the domestic content of the PRC's total exports. Because we are unable to calculate the amount of imported raw materials and energy used in manufacturing exports, we simply exclude the value of these inputs and assume that reported processing imports represent "entire foreign contents" embedded in the PRC's exports. Obviously, this simplification leads to an overestimation of the domestic contents. The estimates, however, can be used as an upper limit to check the accuracy and reliability of the estimates with the input–output approach. We compare the estimates of this study with those of the OECD database from 1995 to 2009. Since processing exports play a critical role in determining the share of domestic contents, we include shares of processing exports in the comparison.

Figure 4.5 shows the comparison year by year. The estimates of the OECD for the years 1995–2007 are much higher than those derived by this study. The differences are significant and more than 18 percentage points for more than half of the estimates. In 2000, according to the OECD, domestic

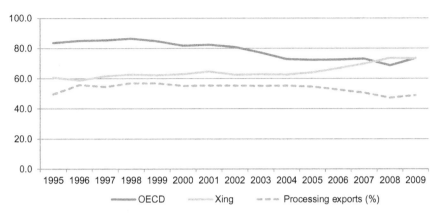

Figure 4.5. Comparison of our estimates with OECD trade in value added (TiVA) estimates.

Note: OECD = Organisation for Economic Co-operation and Development.

Source: OECD TiVA database and author's calculations.

contents made up 81.7% of the PRC's exports, while our estimate suggests 62.9%. Similarly, the OECD concludes that 72.3% of value added of the exports was generated domestically in 2005 and this study finds that the domestic content was no more than 64%. Furthermore, the estimates of the OECD indicate a declining trend of domestic contents from 83.6% to 73.4% from 1995 to 2009. On the contrary, our estimates imply a rising trend from 60.8% to 73.2% over the same period. Moreover, the changing dynamics implied by the estimates of the OECD are inconsistent with those of processing exports. According to the OECD, the domestic value added rose from 83.6% to 86.4% from 1995 to 1999 while the share of processing exports jumped to 57%. By 2009, the share of processing exports dropped to 49%, but the OECD estimate suggests that the domestic content also fell to 73.4%.

As explained earlier, our estimation does not include some basic raw materials and energy inputs imported from abroad, so the estimates of this study represent the upper boundaries of domestic content. If the statistical errors of the OECD estimates are acceptable, the estimates should not deviate too much from our results. Moreover, compared with normal trade, domestic contents of processing exports are lower. As the weight of processing exports gradually decreases, the domestic value added should rise rather than decrease. The trend implied by the OECD estimates is inconsistent with the decline of processing exports. The observed positive correlation between the shares of processing exports and the value added estimated by the OECD contradict the fact that processing exports generally contain less domestic content than normal exports. Therefore, the estimates of the OECD carry substantial statistical error. Relaxing some key assumptions may be necessary to enhance the accuracy of the OECD TiVA data. At the current stage, caution is warranted to apply these estimates for empirical analysis.

4.6. Conclusion

Conventional trade statistics inflate trade flows and distort bilateral trade relations. It is the consensus to measure trade flows in value added by nations involved in GVCs. So far, all available estimates are derived from international input–output tables. The theoretical foundation of the input–output approach has been rigorously established. However, figures obtained from international input–output tables are estimates not actual values. Constructing input–output tables for all countries, including many sectors is a daunting task. The reliability and accuracy of the estimates depends on the estimated coefficients and whether critical features of GVCs are ignored by the assumptions. In this chapter, we introduce a direct approach to calculate the domestic value added of the PRC's processing exports. We prove mathematically that the method can be used to calculate domestic contents without double counting problem. The major pitfall of the method is that imported raw materials and energy inputs are omitted; thus, domestic value added tends to be overestimated. Our estimates should therefore be considered as the upper limits of domestic value added. We also analyze the heterogeneity of the PRC's processing exports over its major trading partners and find that shares of processing exports to high-income economies are generally higher than that to low-income economies, suggesting that the domestic contents vary across destination markets. The comparison between the results of this study and the OECD TiVA database indicates that the OECD substantially overestimates the domestic value added of the PRC's exports and the time trend suggested by the OECD estimates are inconsistent with the fact that the share of processing exports has gradually declined over time.

References*

Hummels, D., J. Ishii, and K. Yi. 2001. The Nature and Growth of Vertical Specialization in the World Trade. *Journal of International Economics* 54: 75–96.

Koopman, R., Z. Wang, and J. We. 2009. A World Factory in Global Production Chains: Estimating Imported Value Added in Chinese Exports. Discussion Paper No. 7430, Center for Economic Policy Research, UK.

Koopman, R., Z. Wang, and S.J. Wei. 2012. The Value-Added Structure of Gross Exports and Global Production Network. Paper presented at the Final WIOD Conference "Cause and Consequences of Globalization," April, Groningen, The Netherlands.

Merri, T. 2009. China Passes the EU in High-Tech Exports. Science and Technology, Eurostat Statistics in Focus. http://epp.eurostat.ec.europa.eu/cache/ITY_OFFPUB/.KS-SF-09-025/EN/KS-SF-09-025-EN.PDF (accessed 24 September 2013).

OECD and WTO (Organisation for Economic Co-operation and Development and World Trade Organization). 2013. Trade in Value-Added: Concepts, Methodologies and Challenges — Joint OECD–WTO Note. http://www.oecd.org/sti/ind/49894138.pdf (accessed 24 September 2013).

Rodrik, D. 2006. What's So Special about China's Exports. NBER Working Paper No. 11947. Cambridge, MA: National Bureau of Economic Research.

Scott, R.E. 2011. The China Toll: Growing US Trade Deficit with China Cost More Than 2.7 Million Jobs between 2001 and 2011, with Job Losses in Every State. EPI Briefing Paper No. 345. http://www.epi.org/publication/bp345-china-growing-trade-deficit-cost/

UNCTAD. 2013. *World Investment Report 2013*. Geneva: United Nations Publication.

Xing, Y. 2014. China's High-Tech Exports: The Myth and Reality. *Asian Economic Papers* 13(1): 109–123.

Xing, Y. 2012. Processing Trade, Exchange Rates and China's Bilateral Trade Balance. *Journal of Asian Economics* 23(5): 540–547.

Xing, Y. and N. Detert. 2010. How the iPhone Widens the United States Trade Deficit with the People's Republic of China. ADBI Working Paper No. 257. Tokyo: Asian Development Bank Institute.

---

*The Asian Development Bank refers to China by the name People's Republic of China.

Chapter 5

An Alternative Measurement for International Fragmentation of the Production Process: An International Input–Output Approach

Satoshi Inomata

This chapter investigates the possibility of constructing an alternative measurement for analyzing the international fragmentation of the production process. It asserts that current usage of relevant information, whether trade shares of parts and components or the index of vertical specialization, is unsatisfactory for measuring the phenomenon, since they critically lack an overall perspective of the entire structure of production chains. A new measurement is formulated that captures every aspect of the vertical sequence of production linkages. It is based on the input–output model of average propagation lengths, which shows the average number of production stages that are passed through for an exogenous change in one industry to affect another. By applying this model to the Asian International Input–Output data, we are able to measure the international dimension of production sharing and division of labor in East Asia.

5.1. Introduction

During the last few decades, there has been flourishing discussion on a new economic phenomenon of international trade. The number of segments in a production process, or production chain, has been rapidly and extensively relocated to different places of different countries. The international fragmentation of the production process caught the interest of many academics and policy makers alike, and various analytical models were formulated thereafter in order to capture the dynamics of this new economic trend.

Prompted by earlier propositions of Ethier (1982), the theoretical side of international fragmentation underwent significant development through a series of studies in the 1990s. Based on the classic concept of comparative advantage, the theory and its major implications became well established and widely shared. What has lagged behind, however, is the empirical analysis. Although relevant data have become increasingly available, the methodological aspect of constructing an appropriate measurement has yet to catch up.

This chapter proposes a new and complementary approach for measuring the international fragmentation of the production process, in order to contribute to the development of empirical analysis on the topics of current concern. The chapter is organized as follows. Section 5.2 briefly reviews previous empirical studies and discusses possible shortcomings of the measurements employed in those studies. In Section 5.3, a new measurement for international fragmentation is introduced, with an explanation of the underlying theoretical model and the basic picture of inter-country input–output data. Section 5.4 presents calculation results using the new measurement and compares the results with other types of indices. Section 5.5 summarizes the discussion.

5.2. Literature Review

5.2.1. *Studies using foreign trade statistics*

Empirical studies in the earliest phase largely relied on information from foreign trade statistics. Following an earlier approach developed in Yeats (1998), Ng and Yeats (1999) set forth a comprehensive analysis of production sharing in the East Asian region. By using trade data for parts and components of 60 manufacturing industries, it asserts that, as of 1996, the increasing share of components trade presents strong evidence for production sharing between countries. East Asia's global exports of components from 1984 to 1996 grew at an annual rate of 15% compared with 11% for all manufacturing products. In particular, intraregional trade rapidly intensified, with its share of total trade almost doubling from 25% to 46%.

While foreign trade statistics are undoubtedly the most accessible data for the study of international trade, and have become increasingly available for many countries, the statistics remain a rather crude proxy for the phenomenon of international fragmentation. They contain no information on the linkages between industries, hence, the vertical structure of the production process, which is supposed to be the analytical target of international fragmentation, cannot be depicted. The import and export values of parts and components offer a suggestion or a "clue" for considering the propensity of international fragmentation, yet it cannot depict the phenomenon *per se*.

5.2.2. *Studies using input–output tables*

Another strand of studies developed along the use of input–output tables. The strength of an input–output table is indeed the information of production linkages that are derived from input–output relations between industries. In this regard, Hummels *et al.* (2001) present a simple yet tractable usage of input–output data, introducing a narrowly defined concept of international fragmentation. They define *vertical specialization* as the amount of intermediate inputs used for the production of a good divided by the total output of that good, multiplied by its export value. Put differently, it is the imported contents of an exported item. Within this input–output framework, a country's vertical specialization is represented in matrix form as VS = $\mathbf{uMx}$, where $\mathbf{u}$ is a summation vector, $\mathbf{M}$ is an import coefficient matrix, and $\mathbf{x}$ is an export vector.

The index of vertical specialization offers significant methodological advances, in the sense that it explicitly incorporates industrial linkages in the specification of the index. By utilizing input–output tables with import matrices, it is able to quantify the international dimension of vertical linkages in the form of import contents embodied in exported items.

The approach was further extended for the analysis of East Asian countries by Uchida (2008), which utilizes data of the Asian International Input–Output Tables for the years 1975–2000.[1] Shrestha (2007) also uses the same dataset for analyzing the East Asian region, though it devises a slightly different framework of vertical specialization.

5.2.3. *Possible shortcomings of present measurements*

Although the studies mentioned above have been repeatedly cited and referred to in a various subsequent research, a close examination of the concept of international fragmentation reveals that present methods do not offer satisfactory measurements to describe the phenomenon.

---

[1]The tables were constructed by the Institute of Developing Economies, Japan External Trade Organization.

The theory of fragmentation predicts that if the production process of a certain final good consists of many segments of production stages, or has potentials for further segmentation by change in economies of scales, then there exists a larger opportunity for a fine division of labor that leads to better allocation of resources and lowers the marginal cost of production. This is especially true if we allow for access to international markets, since differences in factor endowments (and hence comparative advantages) are even more prominent across borders.[2]

It is quite evident, therefore, that the analysis of fragmentation concerns the number of production stages involved in a production process. It is a study that compares alternative technologies that lead to the production of the same good, between one comprising few production stages and another with many.[3] In this sense, the index of vertical specialization is explicit in its limitation; even though it refers to the industrial linkage of certain segments of production chains, it cannot trace back the sequence by any more than two consecutive stages. Vertical specialization, therefore, fails to provide a complete picture of the entire production chain, and is bound to give us only a partial indication of the dynamics of international fragmentation.[4] Empirical research requires an overall perspective of the entire structure of production chains. Not only does the size and/or magnitude of production linkages matter, but also the "length" of the chains, determined by the number of production stages therein, provides important information for analysis.

---

[2]See Jones and Kierzkowski (1990), and Deardorff (1998).

[3]Deardorff (1998) defines "fragmentation" as "the splitting of a production process into two or more steps that can be undertaken in different locations but that lead to the same final product."

[4]Hummels *et al.* (2001) also present an alternative model that incorporates the overall domestic production linkages. The model, $\text{VS} = \mathbf{u}\mathbf{M}(\mathbf{I} - \mathbf{A})^{-1}x$ where $(\mathbf{I} - \mathbf{A})^{-1}$, a Leontief inverse matrix, captures both the direct and indirect effects of the export demand on imports, by allowing domestic circulation of the external impact before it ultimately induces the import of intermediate products.

This does not, however, solve the current problem since the Leontief inverse only gives an *ex post* image of demand propagation but cannot refer to its "process." All individual stages of the production process are "squashed and stamped" into a picture of a static equilibrium. The Leontief inverse in this setting is just a black box regarding the vertical structure of production linkages.

5.3. An Alternative Measurement of International Fragmentation

5.3.1. *The model*

In this section, an alternative measurement for international fragmentation is proposed. The method of constructing the new measurement is based on the model of average propagation lengths, the latest technique of input–output analysis developed in Dietzenbacher *et al.* (2005).

Suppose an n-sector economy with a production structure is defined by the input coefficient matrix **A** shown in Figure 5.1(a). Input coefficients a_{ij} are calculated from an input–output table by dividing input values of goods and services used in each industry by the industry's corresponding total output, $a_{ij} = z_{ij}/X_j$, where z_{ij} is a value of good/service i purchased for the production of industry j, and X_j is the total output of industry j. So, the coefficients represent the direct requirement of inputs for producing just one unit of output of industry j.

The vertical sequence of production spillover can be depicted as follows. Let us consider the impact of demand for 100 units in sector 3 upon the output of sector 1. The simplest form is given by the direct linkage $[3 \to 1]$, which is calculated as a product of multiplying 100 units by input coefficient a_{13}. This is because a_{13}, by definition of an input coefficient, represents an immediate amount of good 1 required for producing just one unit of good 3. Alternatively, there is a two-step path going through another industry, say $[3 \to 2 \to 1]$. This is derived by two-stage multiplication, 100 units by

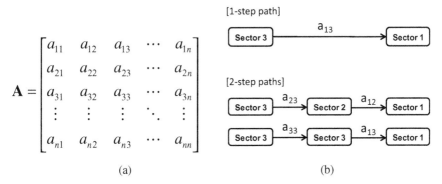

$$\mathbf{A} = \begin{bmatrix} a_{11} & a_{12} & a_{13} & \cdots & a_{1n} \\ a_{21} & a_{22} & a_{23} & \cdots & a_{2n} \\ a_{31} & a_{32} & a_{33} & \cdots & a_{3n} \\ \vdots & \vdots & \vdots & \ddots & \vdots \\ a_{n1} & a_{n2} & a_{n3} & \cdots & a_{nn} \end{bmatrix}$$

(a)   (b)

Figure 5.1. Input coefficient matrix and impact delivery paths. (a) An input coefficient matrix. (b) Impact delivery paths.

a_{23}, and then by a_{12}. There can also be a two-step path going through the same sector, such as $[3 \to 3 \to 1]$ or $[3 \to 1 \to 1]$ which would be derived respectively as "$100 \times a_{33} \times a_{13}$" and "$100 \times a_{13} \times a_{11}$" (Figure 5.1(b)).

The simulation reveals that the impact of any two-step path, whatever the sequence of sectors, can be given by the feedback operation of re-injecting a set of direct impacts back into the input coefficient matrix, $\mathbf{A} \times \mathbf{A} = \mathbf{A}^2$. Similarly, the impact of three-step paths is given by $\mathbf{A}^3$, that of four-step paths by $\mathbf{A}^4$ and so on, which is evident from $[\mathbf{A}^2]_{ij} = \Sigma_k a_{ik} a_{kj}$, $[\mathbf{A}^3]_{ij} = \Sigma_k \Sigma_h a_{ik} a_{kh} a_{hj}, \ldots$ The amount of impact shown in each layer of $\mathbf{A}^k$s ($k = 1, 2, 3, \ldots,$) is a result of the initial demand injection passing through all k-step paths. It captures the effect of every direct and indirect linkage which undergoes exactly the $k$steps of the production process with k segments of production stages.

Meanwhile, it is mathematically known that a Leontief inverse matrix $\mathbf{L}$, which shows the total amount of goods and services required for the production of one unit of output, can be expanded as an arithmetic series, $\mathbf{L} = (\mathbf{I} - \mathbf{A})^{-1} = \mathbf{I} + \mathbf{A} + \mathbf{A}^2 + \mathbf{A}^3 + \mathbf{A}^4 + \cdots$, where $\mathbf{I}$ is an identity matrix (with 1 in diagonal elements and 0 elsewhere) and $\mathbf{A}$ is an input coefficient matrix. From what we saw above, it is immediately clear that the equation represents the decomposition of the total economic impact on output into its constituent layers according to the number of production stages involved. $\mathbf{I}$ is an initial demand injection, and the following $\mathbf{A}^k$s are regarded as progressive impacts of the initial demand when production chains are sliced at the kth stage of the production process.

With this preliminary understanding, average propagation lengths are specified as

$$v_{ij} = 1^* a_{ij}/(l_{ij} - \delta_{ij}) + 2^* [\mathbf{A}^2]_{ij}/(l_{ij} - \delta_{ij}) + 3^* [\mathbf{A}^3]_{ij}/(l_{ij} - \delta_{ij}) + \cdots$$

$$= \sum_{k=0}^{\infty} k \left[\frac{[\mathbf{A}^k]_{ij}}{\sum_{k=1}^{\infty} [\mathbf{A}^k]_{ij}} \right],$$

where $\mathbf{A}$ is an input coefficient matrix, a_{ij} is its element, l_{ij} is a Leontief inverse coefficient, δ_{ij} is a Kronecker delta which is $\delta_{ij} = 1$ if $i = j$ and $\delta_{ij} = 0$ otherwise, and k is the number of production stages along the path. We also define $v_{ij} = 0$ when $(l_{ij} - \delta_{ij}) = 0$.

The first term on the right-hand side of the equation shows that the impact delivered through one-step paths ($k = 1$), direct impact, amounts to an $a_{ij}/(l_{ij} - \delta_{ij})$ share of the total impact given by the Leontief inverse coefficient (less unity for diagonal elements). Similarly, two-step paths ($k = 2$) contribute an $[\mathbf{A^2}]_{ij}/(l_{ij} - \delta_{ij})$ share, and three-step paths ($k = 3$) an $[\mathbf{A^3}]_{ij}/(l_{ij} - \delta_{ij})$ share of the total impact. This is evident from $\mathbf{L} = \mathbf{I} + \mathbf{A} + \mathbf{A^2} + \mathbf{A^3} + \cdots$ which is rearranged as $\mathbf{L} - \mathbf{I} = \mathbf{A} + \mathbf{A^2} + \mathbf{A^3} + \cdots$, and hence $(\mathbf{L} - \mathbf{I})_{ij} = \mathbf{A}_{ij} + [\mathbf{A^2}]_{ij} + [\mathbf{A^3}]_{ij} + \cdots$.

That is, average propagation lengths are formulated as a weighted average of the number of production stages which are passed by an economic impact (for example demand increase) generated in industry j until it ultimately reaches industry n through production networks, using the share of impact at each stage as a weight. It represents the average number of production stages lining up in every branch of all the production chains, or, in short, an industry's level of fragmentation.

Here, the international fragmentation index F is defined as

$$
F_j = \left\{ \boxed{\begin{array}{c} \text{Weighted} \\ \text{average of } v \end{array}} - \boxed{\begin{array}{c} \text{Weighted} \\ \text{average of } v^d \end{array}} \right\} \Bigg/ \boxed{\begin{array}{c} \text{Weighted} \\ \text{average of } v^d \end{array}}
$$

$$
= \left\{ \sum_{i=1}^{mn} v_{ij} \frac{l_{ij} - \delta_{ij}}{\sum_i (l_{ij} - \delta_{ij})} - \sum_{i=1}^{mn} v_{ij}^d \frac{l_{ij}^d - \delta_{ij}}{\sum_i (l_{ij}^d - \delta_{ij})} \right\} \Bigg/ \sum_{i=1}^{mn} v_{ij}^d \frac{l_{ij}^d - \delta_{ij}}{\sum_i (l_{ij}^d - \delta_{ij})}
$$

$$(i = 1, 2, 3, \ldots, mn, \ j = 1, 2, 3, \ldots, mn)^5$$

where

v is average propagation lengths of an inter-country input–output table,
v^d is average propagation lengths of domestic transactions,
l is Leontief inverse coefficients of an intercountry input–output table,
l^d is Leontief inverse coefficients of domestic transactions,
δ is Kronecker delta, i.e., $\delta_{ij} = 1$ if $i = j$, and $\delta_{ij} = 0$ otherwise,
m is number of endogenous countries, and

---

[5]Note that i and j are sequentially numbered in a way that represents the same industry in different countries as different industrial sectors.

n is number of industrial sectors for each country.

v^d represents the degree of domestic division of labor based on the production technique that would be chosen when no trade with other countries is assumed. On the other hand, v represents the degree of international division of labor based on the production technique that would be chosen when the economy is opened to overseas production networks. Therefore, the difference or deviation between these two values, as formulated in the definition above, represents the level of foreign outsourcing within the region of analysis, or the degree of international fragmentation.

Also, the multiplication of v and v^d by the shares of the Leontief inverse coefficients guarantees that the values are weighted in accordance with the linkage effect upon each industry, which is considered to represent the "importance" of the corresponding circuit in the production chain. (The value of one is subtracted from a Leontief inverse coefficient for diagonal elements, in order to negate the initial demand injection since it does not depend upon the economy's industrial structure and hence is not relevant for our analysis).

In constructing the international fragmentation index, the v and v^d values are calculated from two different forms of input coefficient matrices

$$v_{ij} = \sum_{k=1}^{\infty} k \left[\frac{\left[\mathbf{A}^k\right]_{ij}}{\sum\limits_{k=1}^{\infty} \left[\mathbf{A}^k\right]_{ij}} \right],$$

$$v_{ij}^d = \sum_{k=1}^{\infty} k \left[\frac{\left[\mathbf{A}_d^k\right]_{ij}}{\sum\limits_{k=1}^{\infty} \left[\mathbf{A}_d^k\right]_{ij}} \right].$$

Similarly, the Leontief inverse coefficients are given by

$$l_{ij} = \left[(\mathbf{I} - \mathbf{A})^{-1} \right]_{ij} \quad \text{and} \quad l_{ij}^d = \left[(\mathbf{I} - \mathbf{A}_d)^{-1} \right]_{ij}.$$

Matrix $\mathbf{A}$ is the input coefficient matrix of the entire inter-country I–O table, and matrix $\mathbf{A}_d$ is the input coefficient matrix that consists of submatrices of domestic transactions for diagonal parts and null matrices elsewhere

$$\mathbf{A}_d = \begin{bmatrix} \mathbf{A}^{rr} & 0 & 0 & \cdots & 0 \\ 0 & \mathbf{A}^{ss} & 0 & \cdots & 0 \\ 0 & 0 & \mathbf{A}^{tt} & \cdots & 0 \\ \vdots & \vdots & \vdots & \ddots & 0 \\ 0 & 0 & 0 & 0 & \mathbf{A}^{zz} \end{bmatrix},$$

$(r, s, t, \ldots, z$: countries of origin and destination).[6]

Finally, we define

$$F_j = 0, \quad \text{if} \quad \sum_{i=1}^{mn} \left(v_{ij}^d \frac{l_{ij}^d - \delta_{ij}}{\sum_i (l_{ij}^d - \delta_{ij})} \right) = 0.$$

5.3.2. The data

We utilize the Asian International Input–Output Tables for the reference years — 1990, 1995, and 2000 — constructed by the Institute of Developing Economies, Japan External Trade Organization (IDE-JETRO 1990, 1995, 2000). Table 5.1 shows a schematic image of the data. The table links national I–O tables of 10 economies: Indonesia (I), Malaysia (M), the Philippines (P), Singapore (S), Thailand (T), People's Republic of China (C), Taipei,China (N), Republic of Korea (K), Japan (J), and United States (U).[7] Each cell of A** represents transactions among 24 industrial sectors, namely, it is a square matrix of 24 dimensions.[8] The table is

---

[6]Note, therefore, that the Leontief inverse coefficients of domestic transactions matrix are given as:

$$l_{ij}^d = \left[(\mathbf{I} - \mathbf{A}_d)^{-1} \right]_{ij} = \begin{bmatrix} (\mathbf{I} - \mathbf{A}^{rr})^{-1} & 0 & 0 & \cdots & 0 \\ 0 & (\mathbf{I} - \mathbf{A}^{ss})^{-1} & 0 & \cdots & 0 \\ 0 & 0 & (\mathbf{I} - \mathbf{A}^{tt})^{-1} & \cdots & 0 \\ \vdots & \vdots & \vdots & \ddots & 0 \\ 0 & 0 & 0 & 0 & (\mathbf{I} - \mathbf{A}^{zz})^{-1} \end{bmatrix}_{ij}.$$

[7]In what follows, the term "East Asia" includes the United States, except when otherwise specified.

[8]For a description of industrial sector classifications, see Appendix 5A.

Table 5.1. The Asian International Input–Output Table.

	code	Indonesia (AI)	Malaysia (AM)	Philippines (AP)	Singapore (AS)	Thailand (AT)	PRC (AC)	Taipei,China (AN)	Rep. of Korea (AK)	Japan (AJ)	US (AU)	Indonesia (FI)	Malaysia (FM)	Philippines (FP)	Singapore (FS)	Thailand (FT)	PRC (FC)	Taipei,China (FN)	Rep. of Korea (FK)	Japan (FJ)	US (FU)	Export to Hong Kong, China (LH)	Export to EU (LO)	Export to ROW (LW)	Statistical Discrepancy (QX)	Total Outputs (XX)
Indonesia	(AI)	A^{II}	A^{IM}	A^{IP}	A^{IS}	A^{IT}	A^{IC}	A^{IN}	A^{IK}	A^{IJ}	A^{IU}	F^{II}	F^{IM}	F^{IP}	F^{IS}	F^{IT}	F^{IC}	F^{IN}	F^{IK}	F^{IJ}	F^{IU}	L^{IH}	L^{IO}	L^{IW}	Q^{I}	X^{I}
Malaysia	(AM)	A^{MI}	A^{MM}	A^{MP}	A^{MS}	A^{MT}	A^{MC}	A^{MN}	A^{MK}	A^{MJ}	A^{MU}	F^{MI}	F^{MM}	F^{MP}	F^{MS}	F^{MT}	F^{MC}	F^{MN}	F^{MK}	F^{MJ}	F^{MU}	L^{MH}	L^{MO}	L^{MW}	Q^{M}	X^{M}
Philippines	(AP)	A^{PI}	A^{PM}	A^{PP}	A^{PS}	A^{PT}	A^{PC}	A^{PN}	A^{PK}	A^{PJ}	A^{PU}	F^{PI}	F^{PM}	F^{PP}	F^{PS}	F^{PT}	F^{PC}	F^{PN}	F^{PK}	F^{PJ}	F^{PU}	L^{PH}	L^{PO}	L^{PW}	Q^{P}	X^{P}
Singapore	(AS)	A^{SI}	A^{SM}	A^{SP}	A^{SS}	A^{ST}	A^{SC}	A^{SN}	A^{SK}	A^{SJ}	A^{SU}	F^{SI}	F^{SM}	F^{SP}	F^{SS}	F^{ST}	F^{SC}	F^{SN}	F^{SK}	F^{SJ}	F^{SU}	L^{SH}	L^{SO}	L^{SW}	Q^{S}	X^{S}
Thailand	(AT)	A^{TI}	A^{TM}	A^{TP}	A^{TS}	A^{TT}	A^{TC}	A^{TN}	A^{TK}	A^{TJ}	A^{TU}	F^{TI}	F^{TM}	F^{TP}	F^{TS}	F^{TT}	F^{TC}	F^{TN}	F^{TK}	F^{TJ}	F^{TU}	L^{TH}	L^{TO}	L^{TW}	Q^{T}	X^{T}
PRC	(AC)	A^{CI}	A^{CM}	A^{CP}	A^{CS}	A^{CT}	A^{CC}	A^{CN}	A^{CK}	A^{CJ}	A^{CU}	F^{CI}	F^{CM}	F^{CP}	F^{CS}	F^{CT}	F^{CC}	F^{CN}	F^{CK}	F^{CJ}	F^{CU}	L^{CH}	L^{CO}	L^{CW}	Q^{C}	X^{C}
Taipei,China	(AN)	A^{NI}	A^{NM}	A^{NP}	A^{NS}	A^{NT}	A^{NC}	A^{NN}	A^{NK}	A^{NJ}	A^{NU}	F^{NI}	F^{NM}	F^{NP}	F^{NS}	F^{NT}	F^{NC}	F^{NN}	F^{NK}	F^{NJ}	F^{NU}	L^{NH}	L^{NO}	L^{NW}	Q^{N}	X^{N}
Rep. of Korea	(AK)	A^{KI}	A^{KM}	A^{KP}	A^{KS}	A^{KT}	A^{KC}	A^{KN}	A^{KK}	A^{KJ}	A^{KU}	F^{KI}	F^{KM}	F^{KP}	F^{KS}	F^{KT}	F^{KC}	F^{KN}	F^{KK}	F^{KJ}	F^{KU}	L^{KH}	L^{KO}	L^{KW}	Q^{K}	X^{K}
Japan	(AJ)	A^{JI}	A^{JM}	A^{JP}	A^{JS}	A^{JT}	A^{JC}	A^{JN}	A^{JK}	A^{JJ}	A^{JU}	F^{JI}	F^{JM}	F^{JP}	F^{JS}	F^{JT}	F^{JC}	F^{JN}	F^{JK}	F^{JJ}	F^{JU}	L^{JH}	L^{JO}	L^{JW}	Q^{J}	X^{J}
US	(AU)	A^{UI}	A^{UM}	A^{UP}	A^{US}	A^{UT}	A^{UC}	A^{UN}	A^{UK}	A^{UJ}	A^{UU}	F^{UI}	F^{UM}	F^{UP}	F^{US}	F^{UT}	F^{UC}	F^{UN}	F^{UK}	F^{UJ}	F^{UU}	L^{UH}	L^{UO}	L^{UW}	Q^{U}	X^{U}
Freight and Insurance	(BF)	BA^{I}	BA^{M}	BA^{P}	BA^{S}	BA^{T}	BA^{C}	BA^{N}	BA^{K}	BA^{J}	BA^{U}	BF^{I}	BF^{M}	BF^{P}	BF^{S}	BF^{T}	BF^{C}	BF^{N}	BF^{K}	BF^{J}	BF^{U}					
Import from Hong Kong, China	(CH)	A^{HI}	A^{HM}	A^{HP}	A^{HS}	A^{HT}	A^{HC}	A^{HN}	A^{HK}	A^{HJ}	A^{HU}	F^{HI}	F^{HM}	F^{HP}	F^{HS}	F^{HT}	F^{HC}	F^{HN}	F^{HK}	F^{HJ}	F^{HU}					
Import from EU	(CO)	A^{OI}	A^{OM}	A^{OP}	A^{OS}	A^{OT}	A^{OC}	A^{ON}	A^{OK}	A^{OJ}	A^{OU}	F^{OI}	F^{OM}	F^{OP}	F^{OS}	F^{OT}	F^{OC}	F^{ON}	F^{OK}	F^{OJ}	F^{OU}					
Import from the ROW	(CW)	A^{WI}	A^{WM}	A^{WP}	A^{WS}	A^{WT}	A^{WC}	A^{WN}	A^{WK}	A^{WJ}	A^{WU}	F^{WI}	F^{WM}	F^{WP}	F^{WS}	F^{WT}	F^{WC}	F^{WN}	F^{WK}	F^{WJ}	F^{WU}					
Duties and Import Commodity Taxes	(DT)	DA^{I}	DA^{M}	DA^{P}	DA^{S}	DA^{T}	DA^{C}	DA^{N}	DA^{K}	DA^{J}	DA^{U}	DF^{I}	DF^{M}	DF^{P}	DF^{S}	DF^{T}	DF^{C}	DF^{N}	DF^{K}	DF^{J}	DF^{U}					
Value Added	(VV)	V^{I}	V^{M}	V^{P}	V^{S}	V^{T}	V^{C}	V^{N}	V^{K}	V^{J}	V^{U}															
Total Inputs	(XX)	X^{I}	X^{M}	X^{P}	X^{S}	X^{T}	X^{C}	X^{N}	X^{K}	X^{J}	X^{U}															

Note: EU = European Union, PRC = People's Republic of China, ROW = Rest of World, US = United States.

Source: The 2000 Asian International Input–Output Table, Institute of Developing Economies, Japan External Trade Organization.

valued at producer price, except for the import matrices from Hong Kong, China. The European Union (EU) and Rest of the World are valued at cost, insurance, and freight (CIF).

Inter-country I–O tables are simply patchworks of pieces taken from each national I–O table, and they can be read exactly in the same manner as national tables. Each cell in the columns of the table shows input compositions of industries of the respective country. A^{II}, for example, shows the input compositions of Indonesian industries *vis-à-vis* domestically produced goods and services, i.e., the domestic transactions of Indonesia. A^{MI} in contrast shows the input composition of Indonesian industries for the imported goods and services from Malaysia. Cells A^{PI}, A^{SI}, A^{TI}, A^{CI}, A^{NI}, A^{KI}, A^{JI}, A^{UI}, A^{HI}, A^{OI}, and A^{WI} indicate the imports from other countries. BA* and DA* give international freight and insurance as well as taxes on these import transactions.

The 11th column from the left-hand side of the table shows the composition of goods and services that have gone to the final demand sectors of Indonesia. F^{II} and F^{MI}, for example, show respectively the goods and services produced domestically and those imported from Malaysia that flow into Indonesian final demand sectors. The rest of the column is read in the same manner as for the first column of the table.

$L*^H$, $L*^O$, and $L*^W$ are exports (vectors) to Hong Kong, China; the EU; and Rest of the World, respectively. V* and X* are value added and total input/output, as seen in the conventional national I–O table. Q* represents the statistical discrepancies in each row.

5.4. Calculation Results

5.4.1. *Results for international fragmentation in East Asia*[9]

Figure 5.2 presents calculation results by industrial sectors for the reference years 1990, 1995, and 2000. They are aggregate figures for the whole East Asian region (manufacturing sectors only), and the values are averaged across countries using each industry's gross output as weights.

---

[9] In calculating the average propagation lengths, the number of iteration is set at $k = 10$. Yet this covers more than 98% of total impacts for most of the industrial sectors.

F index

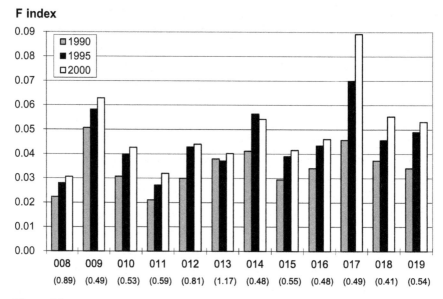

Figure 5.2. International fragmentation in East Asia by industry, 1990–2000.

Note: F index refers to the international fragmentation index.

Source: Calculated by the author using the Asian International Input–Output Tables, 1990–2000.

The capital–labor requirement ratio of each industry is given in parentheses below the sector code.[10]

The industry that showed the highest level of international fragmentation in the year 2000 was machinery, while transport equipment is catching up very rapidly, with a rate of increase of approximately 49%. These findings conform to our intuition that machinery sectors,

---

[10]The capital–labor requirement ratio is calculated from the value added coefficients of the Asian International Input–Output Table using the value added items "wage and salary" and "operating surplus" as proxies. The ratio is defined as k_j/w_j, where k_j and w_j are elements of row vectors $k(\mathbf{I} - \mathbf{A})^{-1}$ and $w(\mathbf{I} - \mathbf{A})^{-1}$ for industry j, respectively, and k and w are the value added coefficient vectors, and $\mathbf{A}$ is the input coefficient matrix, of the inter-country I–O table. (Note that the ratio therefore accounts for the factor requirement of the whole range of production chains of an industry.) The values are averaged across countries using each industry's gross output as weights, and then its period average is taken from the values for 1990, 1995, and 2000.

especially electronics and automobiles, have been playing leading roles in the development of international value chains in East Asia.[11]

The difference in the level of fragmentation seems to be partly attributed to the industry's factor intensity. The average capital–labor requirement ratio of the top five industries (machinery; textiles, leather and products thereof; transport equipment; rubber products; and other manufacturing products) is 0.4807, while the manufacturing sector average is 0.6188, and all-industrial average is 0.7439. This is in line with general predictions of international fragmentation theory in the Heckscher–Ohlin setup, where labor-intensive industries are considered to be more prone to international outsourcing.

Figure 5.3 gives the calculation results for the East Asian economies for reference years 1990, 1995, and 2000. The diagram is designed to compare

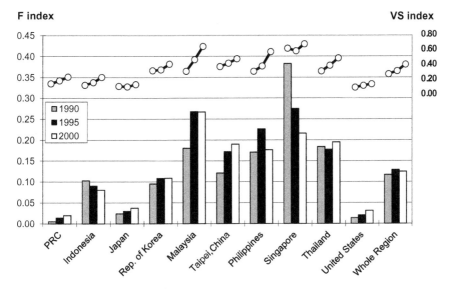

Figure 5.3. International fragmentation in East Asia by economy, 1990–2000.

Note: F index refers to the international fragmentation index, VS index refers to the vertical specialization index.

Source: Calculated by the author using the Asian International Input–Output Tables.

---

[11] See Oikawa (2008).

values of the international fragmentation index and the vertical specialization index in vertical juxtaposition, with the international fragmentation index indicated by the bars at the bottom and the vertical specialization index by the lined-dots on the top.[12] Values are averaged across industrial sectors using each economy's gross output as weights.

The results illuminate the similarities and differences between the international fragmentation index and vertical specialization index. Both indices show the same finding that large economies such as the People's Republic of China, Japan, and the United States have lower figures, while small open economies show larger values. This is in line with the findings of Hummels *et al.* (2001). The difference, on the other hand, can be seen in the trend over time. Looking at the results for the whole region, the vertical specialization index shows a steady increase in values, while for the international fragmentation index the values decline a little from 1995 to 2000. This decline is largely accounted for by the decrease in the index values for Singapore and the Philippines during the period, and a comparison of the values for each of these countries further confirms the difference between the international fragmentation and vertical specialization indices.

Where does the difference come from? We may consider the possibility that these two countries have withdrawn some segments of their production process from regional production networks. This picture echoes with the propositions of Ng and Yeats (1999) about the country profile of the production stage, wherein a comparison of the revealed comparative advantages indices shows that a country may shift from the "assembly stage" to "production stage" for the supply of parts and components as its technological profile develops over time.

Thus, it is possible that Singapore from the early 1990s and the Philippines from the mid-1990s onward started to supply domestically some parts of production inputs, which had previously been purchased from overseas producers. Assembly operations may still be a principal job for them, yet they have successfully "internalized" some segments

---

[12]The vertical specialization index is normalized with respect to each country's volume of export, by using the formula $VS = uM(I - A)^{-1}x^*(1/x)$, where x is the total exports of the country concerned.

of production chains, possibly of upstream industries, after an intensive learning process of the production technology through participation in international production networks.

This possibility, however, can be completely dropped out of the picture drawn by the vertical specialization index. The vertical specialization index is able to shed a light on only a part of production chains, and there is a good chance that the "internalized" segments may rest on the position beyond its analytical range. The international fragmentation index, on the other hand, can grasp it as the model of average propagation lengths captures the entire structure of vertical chains at every production stage of every single branch. The difference in the trend of index values, therefore, seems to reflect the difference in the analytical range of the international fragmentation index and vertical specialization index.

5.4.2. *Comparison with other measurements*

As illustrated in Table 5.2, each index of international fragmentation has its own advantages and disadvantages. For accuracy of measurement, the new index based on average propagation lengths surpasses other types of indices. The data of trade shares consider no vertical linkage, and vertical specialization is able to examine only two consecutive paths, while the new index takes into account every single branch of the production chain in its calculations. For this reason, the new index can display the most accurate picture of international fragmentation.

Table 5.2. Advantages and disadvantages of indices.

	Accuracy of measurement	Calculation requirement	Relevant data availability
Trade shares of parts and components	Low	Light	High (Trade statistics)
Vertical specialization	Intermediate	Light	Intermediate (National input–output table)
Average propagation lengths	High	Heavy	Low (Intercountry table of Isard type)

Source: Constructed by the author.

On the other hand, the new index suffers from the practical problems of data availability and the burden it puts on calculation. Perhaps calculation constraints are not as severe as 10 years ago in terms of data processing capacity. However, since an increasing number of researchers are more used to working on a spreadsheet rather than with a mainframe, users may find out that the current version of the software does not allow inversion of a matrix with a considerably high order. The calculation of the average propagation lengths for a full-scale inter-country I–O table could be a nasty job for them.

The problem of data availability is even more salient. Foreign trade statistics are available for most of the United Nations member countries on a quarterly or monthly basis. Input–output tables are also available for an increasing number of countries since the data constitute the core apparatus of the System of National Accounts (although the release frequency is much lower than the other types of statistics). An inter-country input–output table, by contrast, is rare.

The above notwithstanding, there has been rapid development in data processing capacity and methodological advances for estimating inter-country input–output tables.[13] Previous disadvantages are expected to become less inhibiting for researchers, and hence there is sufficient reason to acknowledge a greater application potential of the new measurement in the years to come.

5.5. Conclusion

This chapter investigated the possibility of constructing a new measurement for the analysis of international fragmentation. It pointed out that the current methods, whether using trade shares of parts and components, or the index of vertical specialization, are unsatisfactory for measuring the phenomenon, since they critically lack an overall perspective of the entire structure of production chains.

A new measurement is formulated such that it captures every aspect of the vertical sequence of production linkages. It is based on the input–output

---

[13]Especially the method developed through the collaboration of the University of Groningen and the Institute of Developing Economies, JETRO, provides a useful reference. See Oosterhaven *et al.* (2008).

model of average propagation lengths, which gives the average number of production stages passed through by an exogenous change in one industry until it ultimately affects another. By applying this model to the data of inter-country input–output tables, this study demonstrated that the index is able to measure the international dimension of production sharing and division of labor.

The results of the empirical study showed that in East Asia, the machinery sector achieved the highest level of international fragmentation between 1990 and 2000, while the cross-national analysis revealed that some countries like Singapore and the Philippines have gradually withdrawn from international production sharing in the region, possibly moving toward a phase of vertical integration of the production process.

A comparison with other types of indices clarified the advantages and disadvantages of the new measurement, but we concluded that the method will overcome current problems in the near future and is expected to open up better prospects for the analysis of international fragmentation.

Appendix 5A. Sector Classification (24 Sectors) of the Asian International Input–Output Table.

Code	Description
001	Paddy
002	Other agricultural products
003	Livestock and poultry
004	Forestry
005	Fishery
006	Crude petroleum and natural gas
007	Other mining
008	Food, beverage and tobacco
009	Textile, leather, and the products thereof
010	Timber and wooden products
011	Pulp, paper, and printing
012	Chemical products

(Continued)

Appendix 5A. (*Continued*)

Code	Description
013	Petroleum and petro products
014	Rubber products
015	Non-metallic mineral products
016	Metal products
017	Machinery
018	Transport equipment
019	Other manufacturing products
020	Electricity, gas, and water supply
021	Construction
022	Trade and transport
023	Services
024	Public administration

References

Deardorff, A.V. 1998. Fragmentation in Simple Trade Models, *Research Seminar in International Economics, Discussion Paper No. 422.*

Dietzenbacher, E., L. Romero, and N.S. Bosma. 2005. Using Average Propagation Lengths to Identify Production Chains in the Andalusian Economy. *Estudios de Economia Aplicada* 23: 405–422.

Ethier, W.J. 1982. National and International Returns to Scale in the Modern Theory of International Trade. *American Economic Review* 72(3): 389–405.

Hummels, D., J. Ishii, and K.-M. Yi. 2001. The Nature and Growth of Vertical Specialization in World Trade. *Journal of International Economics* 54(1): 75–96.

IDE-JETRO. 1990. *Asian International Input–Output Table*, 1990. Tokyo: IDE-JETRO.

IDE-JETRO. 1995. *Asian International Input–Output Table*, 1995. Tokyo: IDE-JETRO.

IDE-JETRO. 2000. *Asian International Input–Output Table*, 2000. Tokyo: IDE-JETRO.

Jones, R.W. and H. Kierzkowski. 1990. The Role of Services in Production and International Trade: A Theoretical Framework. In *The Political Economy of*

International Trade, edited by R.W. Jones and A. O. Krueger. Oxford: Basil Blackwell.

Ng, F. and A. Yeats. 1999. Production Sharing in East Asia; Who Does What for Whom, and Why? Policy Research Working Paper 2197. Washington, DC: The World Bank.

Oosterhaven, J., D. Stelder, and S. Inomata. 2008. Estimating International Interindustry Linkages: Non-survey Simulations of the Asian-Pacific Economy. *Economic Systems Research* 20(4): 395–414.

Oikawa, H.M. 2008. International Value Distribution in Asian Electronics and Automobile Industries: An Empirical Value Chain Approach. IDE Discussion Papers No. 172, IDE-JETRO.

Shrestha, N. 2007. Multi Country Vertical Specialization Dependence: A New Approach to the Vertical Specialization Study. *Hi-Stat Discussion Paper No. 208*. Tokyo: Hitotsubashi University.

Uchida, Y. 2008. Vertical Specialization in East Asia: Some Evidence from East Asia Using Asian International Input–Output Tables from 1975 to 2000. Chosakenkyu-Houkokusho. Tokyo: IDE-JETRO.

Yeats, A.J. 1998. Just How Big Is Global Production Sharing? Policy Research Working Paper 1871. Washington, DC: The World Bank.

Chapter 6

Share of Imports and Commodities in Consumption and Investment in the United States

*Galina Hale and Bart Hobijn**

We use input–output data to compute the share of imports and commodities in personal consumption and fixed investment in the United States (US). We show that for the US, a large high-income economy, the shares of local content and of non-commodity content are rather small in categories that are not directly related to commodities or imported goods. Overall, about 82% of expenditures by US consumers go to goods that are made entirely domestically and from domestic imports. Our measures represent an upper bound on the computed shares of imports from a specific region, because we use a conventional, rather than a value added, measure of trade flows.

6.1. Introduction

The exposure of the United States (US) to the People's Republic of China (PRC) is perceived to be very large, and with good reason: US imports from the PRC in 2011 amounted to 18% of total US imports or 2.6% of US gross domestic product (GDP), with the PRC being the largest source of US imports. What may be less known is that the PRC is also the third largest destination for US exports after Canada and Mexico. US exports to the PRC in 2011 were 7% of US total imports, or 0.7% of US GDP.

However, the perceived impact that the PRC's economic developments have on the US appears to be exaggerated for two reasons. First, these measures of imports and exports are not based on value added and are therefore inflated because of the internationalization of global supply chains

---

*The views are those of the authors and do not necessarily represent those of the Federal Reserve Bank of San Francisco, Federal Reserve System or any other person affiliated with it. This chapter draws heavily from Hale and Hobijn (2011) and Hale *et al.* (2012). We thank Anita Todd for help with preparing this draft.

(see Xing and Detert 2010, as well as Chapter 5 in this volume). Second, local content represents a large portion of US expenditure on imported goods, including goods imported from the PRC.

In this chapter, we focus on the second reason by carefully computing shares of imported goods in total US personal consumption and fixed investment by category. We conduct a similar analysis for the share of commodities to measure the upper bound of US dependence on commodities and imported commodities in particular.

In our analysis, we combine data from the Census Bureau's (2011) US International Trade Data, the Bureau of Labor Statistics' (BLS 2010) input–output matrix, and the personal consumption expenditures (PCE) data from the US national accounts by category. We use the BLS rather than the Bureau of Economic Analysis (BEA) input–output matrix because it better matches the PCE categories of our interest.

One application of our analysis is on the potential for import and commodity prices to pass through to PCE inflation. There is a vast literature measuring pass-through from import and commodity prices using regression analysis. Any statistical analysis, however, is subject to the problem of causality identification. We avoid this problem altogether in our analysis by simply computing the shares of imports and commodity contents in consumption and investment, presenting therefore an upper bound for how much the price increases could pass through to overall price levels. A caveat of our analysis, however, is that it does not take into account price-setting behavior of domestic producers, which could respond to imported price changes by adjusting their prices accordingly.

6.2. Share of Consumer Spending on "Made in China" and Other US Imports

One way the US trade deficit with the PRC manifests itself is in the many items in stores that are labeled "Made in China." In this chapter, we account for what fraction of US PCE is spent on goods labeled "Made in China" and what part of that spending reflects the actual costs of goods imported from the PRC. We repeat this exercise for all imports from the whole East Asian region (excluding Japan) and for all imports into the US. To study this, we address three questions. First, what fraction of spending by US consumers is spent on goods labeled "Made in China" and what fraction is spent on goods "Made in USA"? Second, what part of the cost of such goods is actually due to the cost of the imports from the PRC and what part reflects the value added by US transportation, wholesale, and retail activities, that is, the US content of "Made in China"? We compute similar statistics for "Made in Asia" and for all goods that are not "Made in USA."

Not all imported goods coming from the PRC or other countries get sold directly to US businesses and households. Many of them get used in subsequent stages of production in the US. Thus, our third question is, what part of spending by US consumers can be traced back to the cost of goods imports from the PRC, from Asia overall, and from all other countries, when one takes into account not only the goods sold directly to consumers but also those used as intermediate inputs in goods produced domestically?

To set the stage for our results, it is important to realize that, though globalization is a popular topic these days, the US economy remains relatively closed. That means that the vast majority of goods and services sold in the US are actually produced in the US. In 2010, imports into the US were about 16% of US GDP, with imports from the PRC amounting to 2.5% of US GDP.

This is also borne out in our calculations. As the first number in column (2) of Table 6.1 shows, 88.5% of spending by US consumers is on goods and services made in the US. This is in large part because services, which make up about two-thirds of spending, are mainly locally produced. The market share of foreign goods is the highest in consumption of durable goods, which includes, among others, cars and electronics. Two-thirds of durables consumption in the US is spent on goods that are labeled "Made in USA," while the other third is on goods that are made abroad.

Of the 11.5% that US consumers spend on goods and services not "Made in USA," about a quarter is on goods labeled "Made in China" and about a third on goods labeled "Made in Asia" (which includes the PRC but excludes Japan). "Made in China" goods accounted for 2.7% of spending by US households in 2010 (column (3) of Table 6.1), and consist mainly of electronics, part of "furniture and household equipment" and "other durables," and clothing and shoes. In fact, 35.6% of 2010 US

Table 6.1. Import content of personal consumption expenditure by import origin, 2010.

| | A. Share spent on | | | Import content | | | | | | |
| | | | | B. Directly sold to final demand | | | C. Total content | | | |
	Expenditure Share (1)	"Made in USA" (2)	"Made in China" (3)	"Made in Asia"* (4)	Total (5)	PRC goods (6)	Asian* goods (7)	Total (8)	PRC goods (9)	Asian* goods (10)
Total	100	88.5	2.7	3.7	7.3	1.2	1.7	13.9	1.9	2.8
Less food and energy	86	88.0	3.1	4.1	7.7	1.4	1.9	13.0	2.0	2.9
Durables	10	66.6	12.0	16.0	18.7	6.2	8.3	26.3	7.3	10.1
Motor vehicles	3	74.9	1.2	3.1	17.5	0.6	1.7	27.4	1.9	4.0
Furniture and household equipment	5	59.6	20.0	25.2	21.4	10.6	13.3	27.8	11.6	15.0
Other durables	2	69.0	11.8	16.7	14.2	5.3	7.6	20.5	6.2	9.0
Nondurables	23	76.2	6.4	9.0	12.1	2.6	3.8	22.1	3.3	5.0
Food	8	90.8	0.4	1.2	5.2	0.2	0.7	13.9	1.1	2.2
Clothing and shoes	3	24.9	35.6	45.6	29.5	13.8	17.8	33.6	14.7	19.0
Gasoline, fuel oil, and other energy goods	4	88.4	0.1	1.0	7.4	0.0	0.6	34.1	0.5	1.5
Other nondurables	8	77.7	3.1	5.0	13.8	1.4	2.5	20.1	2.0	3.5
Services	67	96.0	0.0	0.0	4.0	0.0	0.0	9.2	0.6	0.9
Housing	17	100.0	0.0	0.0	0.0	0.0	0.0	2.5	0.4	0.6
Household operations	7	99.7	0.0	0.0	0.3	0.0	0.0	10.6	0.6	1.1
Transportation	2	90.4	0.0	0.0	9.6	0.0	0.0	20.8	0.4	0.8
Medical care	18	99.3	0.0	0.0	0.7	0.0	0.0	6.0	0.6	1.0
Recreation	8	99.6	0.0	0.0	0.3	0.0	0.0	6.6	0.8	1.4
Other services	15	84.3	0.0	0.0	15.7	0.0	0.0	20.2	0.5	0.7

Note: PRC = People's Republic of China. *Asia (excl. Japan) includes the PRC; Republic of Korea; Taipei,China; Malaysia; India; Thailand; Singapore; Indonesia; Philippines; and Hong Kong, China.
Source: Authors' own calculations.

consumer purchases of clothing and shoes were on items with the "Made in China" label. Similarly, looking at all imports from Asia, goods labeled as such account for 3.7% of spending by US households in 2010 (column (4) of Table 6.1), and mostly fall in the same category as "Made in China" goods.

These numbers represent the total share of consumer expenditures on imported goods. Of course, some of this spending goes to the local content of these goods. For example, if one buys a US$70 pair of sneakers made in the PRC, not all of the US$70 spent actually goes to the Chinese manufacturer of the shoes. In fact, the bulk of the price goes to pay for the transportation of these goods in the US, the rent of the store where the item is bought, profits for shareholders in the US retailer, marketing of the sneakers, and, of course, the salaries, wages, and benefits of the US workers who run these operations.

The top number in column (5) of Table 6.1 shows that, of the 11.5% of spending that US consumers do on goods and services produced abroad, 7.3 percentage points are due to the cost of imports. The remaining 4.2 percentage points go to US transportation, wholesale, and retail. Thus, 36% of the price that US consumers pay for imported goods actually goes to US companies and workers.

For imports from the PRC, this fraction is much higher. Whereas goods labeled "Made in China" make up 2.7% of consumer spending, only 1.2 percentage points of this spending actually reflect the costs of the goods imported. This can be seen from the top entry of column (6) of Table 6.1. Thus, on average, of every dollar spent on an item labeled "Made in China," US$0.55 go to locally produced services in the US. Hence, the US content of such items is about 55%. The fact that this is much higher than for all imports is mainly due to higher retail and wholesale margins on consumer electronics and clothing than on most other goods and services. The share of local content for goods that are "Made in Asia" is similar, about 50%, reflecting similar industry composition of imports from Asia overall to those from the PRC.

As mentioned before, not all goods and services that are imported into the US are directly sold to US households. Many are used by US companies in the production of their goods and services. Hence, part of the 88.5% of spending on goods and services "Made in USA" go to imported intermediate goods and services. To properly account for the importance of imports for US consumer spending, one has to take into account the contribution of these imported intermediate inputs. We again use input–output tables to compute the contribution of imports to production of all final goods and services. Combining it with the imported goods and services that are sold directly to consumers yields the total import content of PCE.

Columns (8)–(10) of Table 6.1 list the total import content as a fraction of total spending for overall PCE as well as its subcategories. Column (8) shows that 13.9% of spending by US households can be traced back to the costs of imported goods and services. This is substantially higher than the 7.3% when one ignores imported intermediates. The main contributor to this 6.6%-point difference is imported oil, which makes up a large part of the production cost of "gasoline, fuel oil, and other energy goods" as well as "transportation" services. We will discuss the share of commodities in PCE in the next section of this chapter.

As shown in column (9), the total share of PCE that goes to goods imported from the PRC is 1.9%. The 0.7%-point difference that the inclusion of imported intermediates makes in this case turns out to be mainly due to the use of intermediate goods imported from the PRC in the US production of services. Similarly, as shown in column (10), the total share of PCE that goes to goods imported from Asia as a whole is 2.8%.

To summarize, Figure 6.1 shows the shares of the US PCE that are spent on goods according to where they were produced, taking into account intermediate goods production and local content of imported goods. We can see, once again, that of the 2.7% of purchases that US households spend on goods labeled "Made in China," 1.2 percentage points actually go to the PRC. If we take into account imported intermediate goods, about 1.9% of US consumer spending is attributable to the costs of goods imported from the PRC, while 13.9% is attributable to imports overall.

6.3. Share of Business Spending on "Made in China" and Other US Imports

The earlier discussion still leaves out one category of imported goods, that is, capital goods that are sold as final goods to businesses and are not counted in personal consumption but rather in business fixed investment. We can

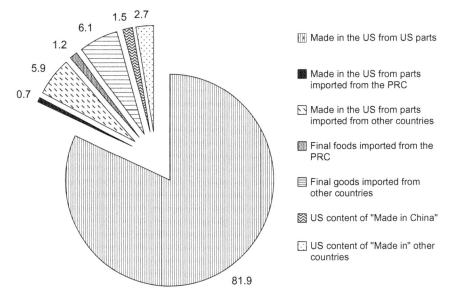

Figure 6.1. Geography of personal consumption expenditures in the United States, 2010.
Note: PRC = People's Republic of China, US = United States.
Sources: Bureau of Economic Analysis, Bureau of Labor Statistics, Census Bureau, and authors' calculations.

use the same approach as above to evaluate the share of imports in fixed investment, as reported in Table 6.2.

Columns (2)–(4) of Table 6.2 show that the share of imports in private fixed investment is larger than the share of imports in consumption, about 22%, of which 5.5% come from the PRC and 8% from Asia overall, excluding Japan. However, as columns (5)–(7) show, the import content of imported investment goods is even smaller than that of consumer goods. Whereas the local component of consumer goods was about 36% for all imports on average, for investment goods this share is about 50%. Unlike for consumer goods, the import content of investment goods coming from the PRC and Asia overall is roughly the same as for an average imported investment good, about 50%.

Columns (8)–(10) of Table 6.2 show the total import content in private fixed investments, including goods that are produced domestically with imported components. Once we account for all these intermediate inputs using the input–output table, we find that about 20% of private fixed

Table 6.2. Import content of private fixed investment by import origin.

	Private fixed Investment Share	A. Share spent on			Import content					
		"Made in USA"	"Made in China"	"Made in Asia"*	B. Directly sold to final demand			C. Total content		
					Total	PRC goods	Asian* goods	Total	PRC goods	Asian* goods
	(1)	(2)	(3)	(4)	(5)	(6)	(7)	(8)	(9)	(10)
Total	100	78.1	5.5	8.1	10.9	2.7	4.1	20.6	4.2	6.4
Equipment and software	59	63.1	9.2	13.7	18.2	4.6	6.8	27.3	5.8	9.0
Computers and software	6	55.9	28.2	34.5	27.7	17.7	21.7	35.5	19.5	24.7
Structures	41	99.9	0.0	0.0	0.1	0.0	0.0	10.8	1.8	2.6
Nonres structures	22	100.0	0.0	0.0	0.0	0.0	0.0	11.4	1.8	2.6
Res structures	19	99.8	0.1	0.1	0.1	0.0	0.0	10.2	1.8	2.6

Note: PRC = People's Republic of China. *Asia (excl. Japan) includes the PRC; Republic of Korea; Taipei,China; Malaysia; India; Thailand; Singapore; Indonesia; Philippines; and Hong Kong, China.
Source: Authors' own calculations.

investment spending goes to imported goods; of that amount, 4.2% goes to goods coming from the PRC, and 6.4% to goods coming from Asia overall. As one would expect, these are primarily in the computers and software category of private fixed investment, a category that accounts for only 6% of private fixed investments.

6.4. Share of Commodities in Consumer Expenditure, and Private Fixed Investment

Commodities such as metals, oil, natural gas, and agricultural products have gone through unprecedented price swings over the past five years. These fluctuations have caused large movements in overall inflation and may have spilled over to core inflation, which excludes food and energy prices.

In this section, which updates results from Hobijn (2008), we calculate the commodity share of US PCE, which is the total outlay for consumer goods and services estimated by the BEA from the same data used to calculate gross domestic product. This share can be traced back to the cost of raw commodities used to produce consumer goods and services. We also compute the share of commodities in private fixed investment. In addition, we isolate the share of imported commodities.

How much of the price of consumer goods and services consists of energy and crop costs? To answer this question, we trace these commodities along the US supply chain for the production of goods and services. We focus on two commodity categories: crops, and oil and gas. We select them because the share in the PCE of all other categories, such as metals, is very small. The crops category consists of fruits and melons, fresh and dried vegetables, nuts, grains, raw cotton, hay, hayseeds, and oilseeds. The oil and gas category includes crude petroleum and natural gas.

For our analysis, we combine 2010 PCE data with the 2008 BLS input–output tables, which are the most recent available. The year 2008 was the peak for real commodity prices, meaning that in 2008, the relative value of commodities was at its highest. Therefore, our estimates of the share of commodities in PCE can be viewed as an upper bound. These estimates are slightly higher than those in Hobijn (2008), which were based on 2006 input–output tables.

Table 6.3. Commodity content of personal consumption expenditure.

	Expenditure share (1)	Commodity content		Imported	
		Crops (2)	Fuel (3)	Crops (4)	Fuel (5)
Total	100	1.3	3.9	0.1	1.9
Less food and energy	86	0.5	1.8	0.0	0.9
Durables	10	0.2	1.3	0.0	0.6
Motor vehicles	3	0.1	0.9	0.0	0.4
Furniture and household equipment	5	0.3	1.5	0.0	0.7
Other durables	2	0.2	1.5	0.0	0.7
Nondurables	23	4.8	8.5	0.2	4.0
Food	8	11.1	2.3	0.6	1.1
Clothing and shoes	3	0.3	1.1	0.0	0.5
Gasoline, fuel oil, and other energy goods	4	0.1	44.8	0.0	20.8
Other nondurables	8	2.6	1.9	0.1	0.9
Services	67	0.3	2.8	0.0	1.3
Housing	17	0.1	0.9	0.0	0.4
Household operations	7	0.1	10.2	0.0	4.9
Transportation	2	0.1	7.1	0.0	3.3
Medical care	18	0.3	2.0	0.0	0.9
Recreation	8	1.3	2.5	0.1	1.2
Other services	15	0.2	1.8	0.0	0.8

Source: Authors' own calculations.

Table 6.3 shows cost shares of crops and oil and gas by consumption expenditures subcategories and the shares of these subcategories in PCE. Oil and gas are important for energy-related expenditures, such as fuel, transportation, and household operations, which include utilities. Crop costs mostly show up in the food subcategory. Outside these areas, commodity-related inputs make up a small part of consumer spending costs. Oil, natural gas, and crops represent around 5% of total consumer expenditures. Of that, oil and natural gas are primary, contributing 3.9 percentage points. As columns (4) and (5) of Table 6.3 show, the share of imports in total expenditures on crops is negligible, while about a half of the expenditures going to fuels ends up going to foreign countries.

Table 6.4. Commodity content of private fixed investment.

	Private fixed investment share	Commodity content		Imported	
		Crops	Fuel	Crops	Fuel
Total	100	0.3	2.8	0.0	1.2
Equipment and software	59	0.1	1.4	0.0	0.7
Computers and software	6	0.1	1.0	0.0	0.5
Structures	41	0.5	4.8	0.0	2.1
Nonres structures	22	0.5	5.2	0.0	2.2
Res structures	19	0.4	4.3	0.0	2.0

Source: Authors' own calculations.

Table 6.4 shows the share of crops and fuel in private fixed investment. Consistent with our findings that the shares of commodities in categories that are not directly related to them are rather limited, we find that the shares of commodities in all fixed investment categories are very small.

6.5. Conclusion

We compute the share of US consumer expenditures and private fixed investments that go to imported goods and to commodities. We find that the shares of imports in both consumer expenditures and in private fixed investments are rather small owing primarily to two factors — a large share of consumer expenditures and fixed investment going to services and real estate, which are inherently non-tradable, and a large share of local content in the total value of imported goods.

It is important, however, not to generalize these results to other countries. While for a large developed economy such as the eurozone the results may be similar (Simola 2012), countries that are smaller or less wealthy are likely to have a larger share of imports in their consumption and investment. Smaller countries are likely to import more intermediate goods than the US or the eurozone, while less wealthy countries tend to have a much smaller share of expenditures on services and non-tradables in general than wealthy countries, due to the Balassa–Samuelson effect.

References*

Bureau of Labor Statistics. 2010. Inter-industry Relationships (Input/Output matrix). http://www.bls.gov/emp/ep_data_input_output_matrix.html.

Census Bureau. 2011. US International Trade Data. http://www.census.gov/foreign-trade/statistics/country/.

Hale, G. and B. Hobijn. 2011. The US Content of "Made in China." *FRBSF Economic Letter* 2011-25 (8 August). http://www.frbsf.org/publications/economics/letter/2011/el2011-25.html.

Hale, G., B. Hobijn, and R. Raina. 2012. Commodity Prices and PCE Inflation. *FRBSF Economic Letter* 2012-14 (7 May). http://www.frbsf.org/publications/economics/letter/2012/el2012-14.html.

Hobijn, B. 2008. Commodity Price Movements and PCE Inflation. *Current Issues in Economics and Finance* 14-8 (November). FRB New York. http://www.newyorkfed.org/research/current_issues/ci14-8.html.

Simola, H. 2012. How Have Emerging Economies Changed Global Price Trends? *Bank of Finland Bulletin* 4-2012.

Xing, Y. and N. Detert. 2010. How the iPhone Widens the United States Trade Deficit with the People's Republic of China. ADBI Working Paper No. 257. Tokyo: Asian Development Bank Institute.

---

*The Asian Development Bank refers to China by the name People's Republic of China.

Chapter 7

Domestic Value Chains
in the People's Republic of China
and Their Linkages with the Global Economy

Bo Meng

Attempts to understand the role of the People's Republic of China (PRC) in global value chains often note the case study of Apple's supply chain, in particular the fact that the PRC contributes no more than 4% of the value added in the production of the iPhone. However, the PRC's share in total induced value added in exports of final products shipped to the United States was more than 75% in 2005. This leads us to investigate how the PRC's value added is created and distributed not only internationally but also domestically. This chapter focuses on measuring domestic value chains (DVCs) in the PRC and their linkages with global markets. By using interregional input–output tables, we can understand structural changes in domestic trade in value added, as well as the position and degree of participation of different regions within the DVCs. We also use our measurements to discuss the PRC's regional economic performance and policy orientation.

7.1. Introduction

The People's Republic of China (PRC) has registered a high rate of economic growth during the last three decades. Its economic scale in real terms expanded more than 2.5-fold from 1987 to 1997, and again from 1997 to 2007.[1] In 2010, the PRC's nominal gross domestic product (GDP) surpassed that of Japan, making it the second largest economy in the world. Domestic forces that have been identified as enabling the PRC to achieve high economic growth are domestic market-oriented economic reforms, ongoing urbanization, industrialization, and regional economic integration.

---

[1] Based on International Monetary Fund statistics, the PRC's GDP at constant price (1990 base) is 1.609 trillion yuan for 1987, 4.149 trillion yuan for 1997, and 10.691 trillion yuan for 2007.

On the international side, the PRC's active participation in global value chains (GVCs) after its accession to the World Trade Organization (WTO) in 2001 has brought about dramatic changes to its own as well as the global economy. Interactions between these forces at both the domestic and international sides provide a powerful engine to support the so-called "China Miracle."

A number of studies have used different approaches to investigate the PRC's role in the increasingly globalized world economy. Recently, case studies examining the PRC's role in Apple's global supply chain (for example Linden *et al.* 2009; Dedrick *et al.* 2010) have received a great amount of attention. In the case of the iPhone, Xing and Detert (2010) show that the PRC contributed only 3.6% of the US$2 billion export to the United States (US), the rest was simply a transfer from Germany, Japan, the Republic of Korea, the US, and other countries. However, if we examine the role of the PRC in global production networks, its share in total induced value added in its exports of final products to the US was about 75% in 2005.[2] This clearly indicates that case studies of iPhone production are specific to a firm and its products, and cannot be generalized to understand the complexity of the PRC's domestic production networks and inter-industrial linkages in the value creation process. As a response to this issue and related topics, some national and international input–output-based analyses have been conducted.[3] However, all of these studies treat the PRC as a single entity rather than considering the expansion of GVCs within the PRC at the regional level. Since there is large variation in the economic size, industrial structure, and overseas dependency across regions within the PRC, we need a regional level perspective to understand the value added creation and distribution mechanisms in detail.

Little research has focused on topics related to the PRC's domestic supply chains and interregional spillover effects by using interregional input–output (I/O) approaches. Zhang and Zhao (2004) investigate spillover

---

[2]This result is based on the author's calculation using the input–output and bilateral trade database of the Organisation for Economic Co-operation and Development.

[3]For example, see Hummels *et al.* (2001), Kuroiwa (2006), Escaith (2008), Koopman *et al.* (2008); Uchida and Inomata (2009), Yang *et al.* (2009), Koopman *et al.* (2010), Degain and Maurer (2010), Fukasaku *et al.* (2011), Johnson and Noguera (2011), Meng *et al.* (2010), Meng *et al.* (2012), Los *et al.* (2012), Stehrer (2012), and Timmer *et al.* (2013).

and feedback effects between coastal and non-coastal regions in the PRC by using the 1997 multiregional I/O table. One important feature of their research is that they distinguish intraregional effects from interregional spillovers at the level of individual industries. Meng and Qu (2008) apply the I/O decomposition technique to the PRC's regional economies for 1987–1997. In their research, a detailed spatial decomposition method is used to explain how spillover and feedback effects of a region contribute to another region's economic growth. Hioki *et al.* (2009) use the I/O-based minimal flow analysis (MFA) to identify structural changes of the PRC's interregional production networks between 1987 and 1997. A clear spatial reorganization of the PRC's supply chains is confirmed in their empirical results. Pei *et al.* (2012) not only pay attention to domestic supply chains, but also use a multiregional I/O model to explain the relationship between regional income disparity and interregional spillover effects. They find that interregional trade and regional income disparities can be partly explained by a region's position in the global supply chain.

Most studies undertaken at the regional level mainly focus on technical decomposition of the interregional Leontief inverse rather than explicitly considering how value is created and distributed in domestic supply chains. Our work differs in this respect, as we focus on elucidating not only the features and evolution of the PRC's domestic value chains (DVCs), but also providing a way to understand the relationship between DVCs and GVCs at the regional level. We apply newly developed GVC-related indicators, such as concepts of vertical specialization (VS), trade in value added (TiVA), and TiVA-based revealed comparative advantage (RCA) to the PRC's regional economies.

The rest of the chapter is organized as follows. Section 7.2 shows how we apply conventional trade indicators such as the vertical specialization, TiVA, and RCA to domestic and regional dimensions. Section 7.3 gives a brief explanation of the database used. Section 7.4 shows the results of the analysis of the PRC's DVCs and its linkages to the global market. Concluding remarks are given in Section 7.5.

7.2. Input–Output-Based Measurement of Value Chains

In this section, we propose new I/O-based indicators for measuring DVCs and their linkages with overseas markets. These indicators include domestic versions of conventional vertical specialization indicators, a measurement of domestic TiVA, and indicators of value added linkages with regard to the contribution of exports to the regional economy. Most ideas in this section can be traced back to traditional I/O-based measurement of GVCs in the existing literature.

7.2.1. *Regional vertical specialization indicators*

To investigate the degree of participation of a region in both domestic and global production networks, we first expand the widely converted vertical specialization indicator (import contents of export) proposed by Hummels *et al.* (2001) into a domestic version. The conventional I/O-based vertical specialization indicator can be written as

$$\text{VS share} = \frac{\mathbf{u} \cdot \mathbf{M} \cdot (\mathbf{I} - \mathbf{A})^{-1} \cdot \mathbf{ex}}{\mathbf{u} \cdot \mathbf{ex}}, \qquad (7.1)$$

where $\mathbf{u}$ is a $1 \times n$ row vector of 1s, $\mathbf{M}$ is the $n \times n$ matrix constructed by using import coefficients (the share of imported intermediate goods in total input), $\mathbf{A}$ is the $n \times n$ domestic input coefficient matrix, $\mathbf{I}$ is an $n \times n$ identity matrix, $(\mathbf{I} - \mathbf{A})^{-1}$ is the domestic Leontief inverse, and $\mathbf{ex}$ is the $n \times 1$ column vector of exports. The above vertical specialization indicator represents intermediate imports directly and indirectly induced by export demand, which can also be explained as the value of imported intermediates embodied in a country's exports. This indicator has been widely used as a proxy to represent the degree of participation of a country in GVCs.

If a single regional I/O table with separate import/export data (foreign trade with the rest of the world) and inflow/outflow data (domestic trade with the rest of the nation) is available, the above national vertical specialization indicator can be expanded to the following four types of regional indicators: (i) regional import contents of export (RIMCE), (ii) regional import contents of outflow (RIMCO), (iii) regional inflow contents of export (RINCE), and (iv) regional inflow contents of outflow (RINCO). In addition, indicators (ii) and (iv) can further yield four indicators if the inflow/outflow information can be separated into trade in intermediate and final products.

The advantages of the above regional vertical specialization indicators include: (i) the degree of participation of a region in domestic and global supply chains can be evaluated, (ii) economic interdependency or interaction between domestic and international supply chains can be measured at the regional level, and (iii) the relative position of a region in both domestic and international supply chains can be identified by focusing on intermediate and final products separately.

7.2.2. *Measuring domestic trade in value added*

To investigate DVCs and their evolution in detail, we apply the concept of global TiVA (Johnson and Noguera 2009) to a domestic interregional I/O framework. Domestic TiVA at the regional level can be simply defined as one region's value added induced by another region's final demand or one region's value added exported to the other region.

To explain the concept of domestic TiVA, we model a closed economy with two regions (r and s) and n sectors for each region. Based on the traditional interregional I/O model, the total value added can be written in the following form:

$$va = diag(v) \cdot L \cdot fd, \tag{7.2}$$

$$va = \begin{pmatrix} va^r \\ va^s \end{pmatrix}, \quad v = (v^r, v^s), \quad L = \begin{pmatrix} L^{rr} & L^{rs} \\ L^{sr} & L^{ss} \end{pmatrix} = \left[I - \begin{pmatrix} A^{rr} & A^{rs} \\ A^{sr} & A^{ss} \end{pmatrix} \right]^{-1},$$

$$fd = \begin{pmatrix} fd^{rr} \\ fd^{sr} \end{pmatrix} + \begin{pmatrix} fd^{rs} \\ fd^{ss} \end{pmatrix}.$$

Here, va^r is the $(n \times 1)$ column vector representing region r's value added by sector, v^r is the $(1 \times n)$ row vector of value added ratio (value added share in total input) by sector for region r, L is the interregional Leontief inverse constructed by the submatrix L^{rs}. A^{rs} represents the $(n \times n)$ matrix of interregional input coefficients from region r to region s, and fd^{rs} is the $(n \times 1)$ column vector representing region s's final demand for goods and services produced in region r. Following the definition of global TiVA, we can formulate region r's value added exported to region s as follows:

$$TiVA^{rs} = (u, u) \cdot diag(v^r, 0) \cdot \begin{pmatrix} L^{rr} & L^{rs} \\ L^{sr} & L^{ss} \end{pmatrix} \cdot \begin{pmatrix} fd^{rs} \\ fd^{ss} \end{pmatrix},$$

$$= v^r \cdot L^{rr} \cdot fd^{rs} + v^r \cdot L^{rs} \cdot fd^{ss}, \tag{7.3}$$

where TiVA^{rs} represents region r's value added induced by region s's final demands on products produced in both the foreign region ($\mathbf{fd}^{rs}$) and the home region ($\mathbf{fd}^{ss}$). Therefore, this type of TiVA can be considered demand-based TiVA from the viewpoint of region s (demander). TiVA^{rs} can be further separated into two parts, concerning different types of final demands, $\mathbf{fd}^{rs}$ and $\mathbf{fd}^{ss}$.

At the product (sector) level, we can regard the induced value added in a specific sector j of region r by a specific final demand for product i in region s as "an individual TiVA linkage," which is defined as:

$$\text{TiVA}_{ij}^{rs} = \mathbf{v}_j^r \left(\mathbf{L}^{rr} \cdot \mathbf{fd}_i^{rs} + \mathbf{L}^{rs} \cdot \mathbf{fd}_i^{ss} \right). \tag{7.4}$$

Based on the above definition, region r's export of sector j's value added to region s (TiVA$_{\cdot j}^{rs}$) can be expressed as

$$\text{TiVA}_{\cdot j}^{rs} = \sum_i \text{TiVA}_{ij}^{rs}. \tag{7.5}$$

In an interregional trade system, a region's products shipped to a partner region may embody a third region's parts and components. Thus, when we consider net trade among regions, conventional interregional trade model cannot provide a reasonable measure because of double counting. This is why we propose to use the concept of TiVA to examine DVCs.

In addition, if we use the following measurement (SP), a region's value added that is incorporated into a partner region's exports can be also measured. This can facilitate our understanding of how a certain region participates in GVCs by acting as a provider of intermediate products in other regions' DVCs:

$$SP^{rs} = (\mathbf{u}, \mathbf{u}) \cdot \text{diag}(\mathbf{v}^r, \mathbf{0}) \cdot \begin{pmatrix} \mathbf{L}^{rr} & \mathbf{L}^{rs} \\ \mathbf{L}^{sr} & \mathbf{L}^{ss} \end{pmatrix} \cdot \begin{pmatrix} \mathbf{0} \\ \mathbf{ex}^s \end{pmatrix}. \tag{7.6}$$

7.2.3. *Alternative measure of regional comparative advantage*

To evaluate a region's comparative advantage at value creation in DVCs, we can apply the concept of domestic TiVA to the measure of regional RCA at the sector level. The concept of RCA is based on the theory of Ricardian comparative advantage. The most widely used indicator of RCA is given as follows (Balassa 1965):

$$RCA_i^R = \frac{EX_i^R / \sum_i EX_i^R}{\sum_R EX_i^R / \sum_R \sum_i EX_i^R},$$ (7.7)

where EX_i^R represents country r's exports of product i. This indicator represents the relative advantage or disadvantage of a country in international trade for a certain class of goods or services. However, as mentioned above, when intermediate imports are used in the production of exports, this indicator may lose its original meaning. Since a region's value added in a specific sector as exported to other regions can be measured by $TiVA_{.j}^{rs}$, we can use this concept to measure a region's comparative advantage of a specific sector at value creation in DVCs in the following way[4]:

$$RCA_{.j}^{r*} = \frac{TiVA_{.j}^r / \sum_j TiVA_{.j}^r}{\sum_r TiVA_{.j}^r / \sum_r \sum_j TiVA_{.j}^r}.$$ (7.8)

7.3. Data Sources

The main data sources used in this chapter for the calculation of domestic TiVA are the PRC's 2002 and 2007 multiregional I/O (MRIO) tables. The MRIO tables were compiled by the State Information Center (SIC) of the PRC in 2012 (Zhang and Qi 2012). Region and sector classifications are shown in Appendix 7A. It should be noted that the import item is a stand-alone vector in the MRIO tables rather than a separate matrix. To calculate the regional vertical specialization indicator as mentioned in the previous section, we use the so-called "same proportion assumption" to transfer the import vector to the import matrix.

7.4. Empirical Analysis

In this section, we first examine the general state of the PRC's regional economies by using regional value added and interregional trade information obtained from 2002 and 2007 MRIO data. Second, we present region-level vertical specialization indicators to show the degree of participation

---

[4]In addition, the bilateral RCA considering a specific target region can also be defined as the following form: $RCA_{.j}^{rsA} = \frac{TiVA_{.j}^{rs} / \sum_j TiVA_{.j}^{rs}}{\sum_r TiVA_{.j}^{rs} / \sum_r \sum_j TiVA_{.j}^{rs}}$. The bilateral RCA provides us with more views for the evaluation of region's comparative advantage.

and position of a certain region in both domestic and international supply chains. Third, we calculate the results of domestic TiVA for 2002 and 2007 in order to illustrate the evolution of interregional value added trade within the PRC's multi-regional value chains. We also use sector-level results of TiVA to evaluate the comparative advantage of different sectors across regions. Finally, regional value added induced by foreign trade is presented to show linkages between the PRC's DVCs and the global market.

7.4.1. *Regional economies and interregional trade*

As an overall view of the evolution of the PRC's regional economies between 2002 and 2007, we calculate the regional value added and its real growth rate by sector. Table 7.1 displays the results. At the national level, total value added increased by 70% over a 5-year period. This is not surprising and corresponds to the PRC's average annual GDP growth rate of roughly 11%.[5] However, the growth rate of value added at the region and sector levels reveal large variations. At the regional level, the northwest, the largest energy-base region, exhibits the highest growth rate at 95%, followed by the two developed coastal regions, the north coast and the east coast with the same levels of growth rate — 79%. The north municipalities, one of the quickly expanding urban agglomeration areas, also exhibit a higher growth rate at 73%. The growth rates of the central region (68%), the southwest (65%), and the south coast (64%) are close to the national average (71%), while the northeast (55%) exhibits a relatively low performance in value added growth.

By comparing regions to the national average as shown in the lower part of Table 7.1, we can identify the leading regions for value added growth by sector. For example, the coastal regions (north and east) can be considered leading regions because their growth rates for most sectors are higher than the national average. The bottom of Table 7.1 displays sectors that are most important to regional economic growth. Manufacturing sectors such as other manufacturing products, non-metallic mineral products, metal products, electric appliances and electronics, and transport equipment play

---

[5]If the annual growth rate of GDP is 11.2% across five years and the first year GDP is 100, the fifth year GDP can be calculated as $(1 + 11.2\%)^5 \times 100 = 170$. This means the 5-year GDP growth rate is simply $(170 - 100)/100 = 70\%$.

Table 7.1. Value added by sector and region and its growth rate.

Billion Chinese yuan (base year: 2002)	Agriculture	Mining and quarrying	Food products and tobacco	Textile and garment	Wood products and furniture	Pulp, paper, and printing	Chemical	Non-metallic mineral products	Metal products	General machinery	Transport equipment	Electric appliances and electronics	Other manufacturing products	Electricity, gas, and water supply	Construction	Trade and transportation	Other services	Total	Share by region (%)
2002																			
Northeast	152	134	37	15	12	12	77	3	59	38	37	21	13	47	60	166	276	1,158	9.5
North	19	18	11	8	1	9	33	4	17	13	9	41	8	12	35	77	317	632	5.2
Municipalities																			
North Coast	253	107	114	58	8	41	114	37	77	72	23	27	21	48	81	194	396	1,673	13.7
East Coast	202	21	59	163	16	52	182	29	109	103	67	143	53	84	116	323	695	2,415	19.8
South Coast	194	43	46	73	35	61	100	22	57	39	25	156	40	66	76	293	554	1,881	15.4
Central	441	159	92	52	26	38	105	62	113	67	48	33	33	89	139	295	582	2,373	19.5
Northwest	126	67	17	8	2	7	30	10	32	11	10	8	5	34	66	103	228	766	6.3
Southwest	276	47	74	9	7	19	45	23	53	22	33	17	11	51	87	160	354	1,286	10.6
Total	1,663	597	450	386	108	237	686	191	517	365	253	445	185	432	659	1,610	3,402	12,186	100.0
Share by sector (%)	13.6	4.9	3.7	3.2	0.9	1.9	5.6	1.6	4.2	3.0	2.1	3.6	1.5	3.5	5.4	13.2	27.9	100.0	
2007																			
Northeast	225	200	57	21	16	9	147	30	82	64	91	26	35	55	100	235	402	1,795	8.6
North	16	43	15	8	2	6	48	7	46	32	27	63	23	32	54	156	519	1,097	53
Municipalities																			
North Coast	336	230	148	115	51	44	215	119	199	130	71	68	49	91	147	322	662	2,997	14.3
East Coast	232	21	105	265	38	66	315	68	272	235	127	319	171	119	211	527	1,224	4,313	20.6
South Coast	243	56	76	166	35	75	177	78	119	71	60	291	93	130	127	374	909	3,078	14.7
Central	605	219	197	94	50	54	225	130	278	121	58	81	77	155	250	462	933	3,990	19.1
Northwest	194	244	54	13	4	7	67	26	107	19	15	13	5	75	107	187	362	1,498	7.2
Southwest	400	71	145	20	10	18	90	35	125	46	56	36	26	97	144	247	557	2,121	10.2
Total	2,250	1,084	798	702	206	279	1,284	491	1,226	718	505	897	479	753	1,139	2,509	5,569	20,889	100.0
Share by sector (%)	10.8	5.2	3.8	3.4	1.0	1.3	6.1	2.4	5.9	3.4	2.4	4.3	2.3	3.6	5.5	12.0	26.7	100.0	

(Continued)

Table 7.1. (*Continued*)

Real growth rate (%)

Billion Chinese yuan (base year: 2002)

	Agriculture	Mining and quarrying	Food products and tobacco	Textile and garment	Wood products and furniture	Pulp, paper, and printing	Chemical	Non-metallic mineral products	Metal products	General machinery	Transport equipment	Electric appliances and electronics	Other manufacturing products	Electricity, gas, and water supply	Construction	Trade and transportation	Other services	Total	Share by region (%)
Northeast	48	50	56	43	34	(21)	91	1,077	37	70	145	24	165	16	67	42	45	55	
North Municipalities	(12)	139	34	(3)	5	(28)	45	83	169	155	199	55	173	170	54	102	64	73	
North Coast	33	115	30	98	524	8	89	217	159	80	209	157	127	89	81	66	67	79	
East Coast	15	1	80	63	140	27	73	13!	150	127	90	124	224	41	82	63	76	79	
South Coast	25	28	65	126	(2)	23	76	246	109	83	138	87	132	97	68	28	64	64	
Central	37	38	115	80	90	44	114	109	147	80	21	147	134	74	80	57	61	68	
Northwest	54	263	213	70	132	2	123	147	230	68	49	48	4	116	61	82	59	95	
Southwest	45	50	97	128	48	(3)	102	52	135	111	66	111	133	88	66	54	58	65	
Total	35	82	78	82	91	18	87	157	137	97	100	102	158	74	73	56	64	71	

Relative to regional average

	Agriculture	Mining and quarrying	Food products and tobacco	Textile and garment	Wood products and furniture	Pulp, paper, and printing	Chemical	Non-metallic mineral products	Metal products	General machinery	Transport equipment	Electric appliances and electronics	Other manufacturing products	Electricity, gas, and water supply	Construction	Trade and transportation	Other services	Total
Northeast	+	−	−	−	−	−	+	+	−	−	+	−	+	−	−	−	−	−
North Municipalities	−	+	−	−	−	−	−	−	+	+	+	−	+	+	−	+	−	+
North Coast	−	+	−	+	+	−	+	+	+	−	+	+	−	+	+	+	+	+
East Coast	−	−	+	−	+	+	−	−	+	+	−	+	+	−	+	+	+	+
South Coast	−	−	−	+	−	+	−	+	−	−	+	−	−	+	−	−	+	−
Central	+	−	+	−	+	+	+	−	+	−	−	+	−	−	+	+	−	−
Northwest	+	+	+	−	+	−	+	−	+	−	−	+	−	+	+	+	−	+
Southwest	+	−	+	+	−	−	+	−	−	+	−	+	−	+	−	−	−	−

(*Continued*)

Table 7.1. (*Continued*)

Billion Chinese yuan (base year: 2002)	Agriculture	Mining and quarrying	Food products and tobacco	Textile and garment	Wood products and furniture	Pulp, paper, and printing	Chemical	Non-metallic mineral products	Metal products	General machinery	Transport equipment	Electric appliances and electronics	Other manufacturing products	Electricity, gas, and water supply	Construction	Trade and transportation	Other services	Total	Share by region (%)
Northeast	−	−	+	−	−	−	+	+	−	+	+	−	+	−	+	−	−		
North Municipalities	−	+	−	−	−	−	−	+	+	+	+	−	+	+	−	+	−		
North Coast	−	+	−	+	+	−	+	+	+	+	+	+	+	+	+	−	−		
East Coast	−	−	+	−	+	−	−	+	+	+	+	+	+	−	+	−	−		
South Coast	−	−	+	+	−	−	+	+	+	+	+	+	+	+	+	−	+		
Central	−	−	+	+	+	−	+	+	+	+	−	+	+	+	+	−	−		
Northwest	−	+	+	−	+	−	+	+	+	−	−	−	−	+	−	−	−		
Southwest	−	−	+	+	−	−	+	−	+	+	+	+	+	+	+	−	−		
Total	−	+	+	+	+	−	+	+	+	+	+	+	+	+	+	−	−		

Relative to sectoral average

Source: Author's own calculations.

a leading role in most regions. This implies that a similar economic growth pattern exists across regions. However, a relatively clear trend toward specialization appears for primary and household consumption products. For example, mining and food sectors in the northwest, textiles in the south coast and southwest, and wood products in the north coast exhibit high growth rates relative to other regions.

The dynamics and diversity of regional and sectoral economic growth depend not only on changes in intraregional production technology but also on interregional production networks (including linkages to overseas markets). In Figure 7.1, the size of the bubbles represents the share of bilateral trade in total interregional trade in 2002 and 2007. To focus on the magnitude of interregional trade, this figure excludes intraregional trade and considers the rest of the world (ROW) as one region. There are no significant structural changes in interregional trade pattern during this 5-year period. Exports and imports of the coastal regions account for a relatively large share. Interactions among coastal regions and between coastal and central regions are the most important elements of domestic interregional trade. However, a careful comparison of the results from 2002 and 2007 can help us conclude a number of interesting differences. For example, in 2007, the east coast replaced the south coast as the leading region in export and import

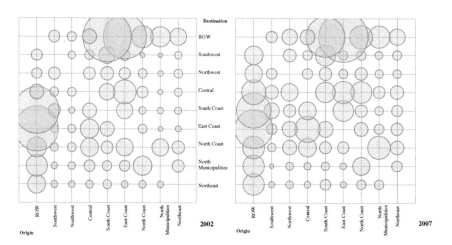

Figure 7.1. Share of bilateral trade in total inter-regional trade, 2002 and 2007.
Note: ROW = Rest of World.
Source: Author's own calculations.

markets. Interactions between the north municipalities and its neighbor region, the north coast, also exhibit a dramatic increase during these five years. The northwest clearly exhibits an increasing magnitude of outflow to coastal regions, as do the coastal regions to the central region. This makes the overall transaction between regions more flat in general (with most small bubbles in 2002 growing larger in 2007).

To investigate the degree of dispersion or concentration of interregional trade at the sector level, we calculate the coefficient of variation (CV) for intermediate and final products separately by sector. The CV is defined as the ratio of the standard deviation to the mean of a dataset and is a normalized measure of the dispersion of data points in a data series around the mean. It is a useful statistic for comparing the degree of variation from one data series to another, even if the means are drastically different. In our data, a higher CV indicates a higher concentration of trade. According to the results displayed in Table 7.2, there are two important features of the changing patterns of interregional trade. First, the concentration of total trade in intermediate products across regions decreased (CV fell from 1.03 to 0.97). However, at the sector level, we confirm a wide variation in the change of the concentration degrees reflecting the increasing complexity of interregional production networks in the PRC. Second, for most final products, the concentration of interregional flows increased rapidly, implying that more regions tend to specialize in production or procurement of final products within the domestic supply chains.

7.4.2. *Region-level vertical specialization trade*

Figure 7.2 shows the regional vertical specialization indicators for 2002 and 2007. At the absolute level, the north municipalities, the east coast, and the south coast have higher (more than 25% in 2007) regional import contents of export (RIMCE) compared with the inland regions and the north coast. The east and south coasts are foreign export-oriented areas with large-scale export processing zones. Manufacturing of export products in these regions are known to use more imports as parts and components by the so-called double-overseas companies.[6] This is why these two coastal

---

[6]Double-overseas companies represent firms that buy raw materials, parts, and components from abroad and sell manufactured goods on the international market.

Table 7.2. Coefficient of variation of interregional trade in intermediate and final products.

Sector	Intermediate products			Final products		
	2002	2007	Change rate (%)	2002	2007	Change rate (%)
Agriculture	1.68	1.81	7.5	1.66	1.77	7.0
Mining and quarrying	1.51	1.65	9.5	2.54	2.43	−4.2
Food products and tobacco	1.62	1.29	−20.6	1.29	1.45	12.2
Textile and garment	1.76	1.56	−11.3	1.57	3.40	117.2
Wood products and furniture	1.70	1.78	4.4	1.86	1.76	−5.5
Pulp, paper, and printing	1.84	1.78	−3.0	1.76	3.46	96.1
Chemical	1.37	1.18	−13.8	1.19	1.32	10.7
Non-metallic mineral products	1.99	1.79	−9.9	1.87	2.06	10.1
Metal products	1.29	1.42	10.0	1.51	1.76	16.6
General machinery	1.80	1.67	−7.6	1.81	2.07	14.2
Transport equipment	1.37	1.37	0.4	1.51	1.61	6.2
Electric appliances and electronics	1.65	2.43	47.8	1.83	2.19	19.6
Other manufacturing products	1.87	1.66	−11.4	1.70	2.05	20.5
Electricity, gas, and water supply	2.21	1.90	−13.9	1.96	2.45	24.9
Construction	2.39	2.00	−16.4	1.99	1.77	−11.0
Trade and transportation	1.23	1.36	10.5	1.27	1.65	29.5
Other services	1.76	2.15	22.7	1.91	2.42	27.0
Total products	1.03	0.97	−5.7	0.98	1.11	12.9

Source: Author's own calculations.

regions have higher vertical specialization figures. It comes as no surprise that the north municipalities, given their low economic self-sufficiency and high dependency on external markets, have a higher RIMCE. Although a coastal region, the main products of the north coast are concentrated in primary sectors such as agriculture, which require fewer imported inputs for production. Therefore, the north coast shows a level of vertical specialization similar to that of the inland regions. Looking at the evolution of RIMCE between 2002 and 2007, the north municipalities and the east coast are leveling off, while the south coast shows a significant decreasing trend. The evolution of the south coast may reflect the ongoing industrial

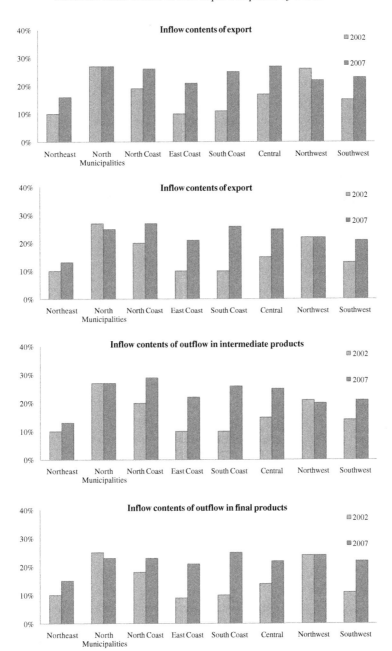

Figure 7.2. Vertical specialization indicator at the regional level, 2002 and 2007.
Source: Author's own calculations.

upgrade process. Namely, this region has been expanding its production linkages to much more inland regions rather than just concentrating in the export-oriented production of processing and assembling goods. On the other hand, the increasing production capacity in terms of intermediate goods in inland regions also provides possibilities for coastal regions to replace imported goods with inflow goods when they take part in GVCs. Another point to note is that the RIMCE figures for all inland regions show significant increases. This implies that the inland regions have been increasingly involved in international supply chains. The most probable explanations for this phenomenon include the following: (i) Most inland regions come to realize the importance and possibilities of the export-oriented economic growth pattern that has been so successful in the coastal regions; (ii) the accession to the WTO provides opportunities not only to coastal regions but also to inland regions to access the world market; and (iii) continuous improvement of the PRC's domestic transportation and logistics systems has increased the accessibility of the inland regions to foreign markets.

Figures for regional import contents of outflow (RIMCO) for most regions are only slightly lower than the figures for RIMCE, and show similar patterns of change. This indicates that import of intermediate products gain importance not only when regions produce products for exports, but also when regions produce goods and services for other domestic regions. In addition, we can see that producing intermediate products for outflow requires more import content in most regions when compared to the figure of RIMCO for final products. This provides evidence that the increase of RIMCO for the east coast and the decline of RIMCO for the north municipalities are mainly due to the contribution of RIMCO for intermediate products.

Looking at the figures for the regional inflow contents of export (RINCE), we can confirm that most regions show large increase between 2002 and 2007, except for the north municipalities and the northeast that were already at very high levels in 2002. This implies that most regions expanded domestic upstream production linkages as they increased their participation in global supply chains. A similar change can be found in the figures for regional inflow contents of outflow (RINCO). Namely, most regions also increased their participation in domestic supply chains.

Examining the differences between RINCO for intermediate products and final products, we see that the north coast's increasing participation in domestic supply chains is mainly due to their growing presence in the production networks of intermediate products. However, for the southwest, the main contribution is from the increasing production of final products.

7.4.3. *Domestic trade in value added*

In the previous section, we calculated the regional vertical specialization indicator to measure participation of a specific region in the PRC's domestic supply chains. This indicator can be estimated if the regional I/O table is available. However, it is difficult to show the structure of DVCs in detail, since interregional spillover and feedback effects in production networks cannot be explicitly captured by using a single regional I/O table. In this section, we apply the concept of domestic TiVA as defined in equation (7.3) to the PRC's MRIO tables for 2002 and 2007. The results of TiVA related indicators can shed light on how value added is created and distributed across regions through interregional production networks.

To check differences in interregional flow of value between the traditional gross term measure (interregional trade) and net term measure (TiVA), we show both results in Table 7.3 for 2002 and 2007. We can see that TiVA (middle part of Table 7.3) is smaller than the figure for traditional trade statistics. This reflects the problem of double counting that occurs in traditional trade statistics when measuring trans-regional flow of value. For ease of comparison, we calculate the share of interregional TiVA in interregional trade. We note large variations across regions. For example, the north coast's export of value added to the southwest region accounts for 93.6% of its exports. This means that only a small amount of value added of other regions is embodied in the north coast's exports to the southwest in 2002. However, the east coast's export of value added to the south coast accounts for just 39.48% of its real flow of products in 2002. This suggests that products produced in the east coast and then shipped to the south coast include a large share of another region's parts and components. If we compare these shares between 2002 and 2007, we see that almost all figures decreased as the national total dropped from 57.21% to 44.85%. This means that most regions have been involved in DVCs and the level of the PRC's domestic market integration has increased.

Table 7.3. Comparison of interregional trade and interregional trade in value added, 2002 and 2007.

	2002								
	NE	NM	NC	EC	SC	CE	NW	SW	Total
	Interregional trade (billion Chinese yuan, current price)								
Northeast	0.00	69.54	74.86	16.49	24.38	31.06	37.70	26.47	280.50
North Munici-pality	19.03	0.00	135.56	11.18	19.26	13.85	14.44	10.37	223.69
North Coast	26.91	166.07	0.00	38.15	26.48	60.93	39.51	11.37	369.42
East Coast	22.62	53.52	137.25	0.00	128.93	256.71	60.66	54.86	714.55
South Coast	36.38	46.24	71.94	100.92	0.00	125.00	84.08	130.02	594.58
Central	29.50	59.16	153.83	163.82	94.95	0.00	66.43	41.50	609.19
Northwest	21.05	24.54	37.72	33.07	18.75	35.79	0.00	27.62	198.54
Southwest	23.28	20.56	34.41	31.67	74.28	38.51	70.59	0.00	293.29
Total	178.75	439.63	645.59	395.3	387.03	561.85	373.41	302.20	3283.76
	Interregional TiVA (billion Chinese yuan, current price)								
Northeast	0.00	38.65	44.37	10.35	13.88	22.77	27.34	20.96	178.33
North Munici-palities	8.31	0.00	61.69	3.94	4.31	7.67	8.22	7.22	101.36
North Coast	18.05	80.29	0.00	19.26	13.56	38.85	26.98	10.64	207.64
East Coast	14.50	29.84	77.42	0.00	50.91	135.24	41.03	43.73	392.67
South Coast	17.78	20.78	37.18	36.44	0.00	64.11	44.69	71.62	292.60
Central	23.23	40.85	89.42	91.98	49.04	0.00	51.74	36.57	382.83
Northwest	13.32	14.66	22.71	16.24	9.67	23.70	0.00	19.70	120.01
Southwest	17.95	15.61	26.26	20.71	38.05	32.22	52.26	0.00	203.05
Total	113.15	240.67	359.05	198.92	179.42	324.56	252.26	210.44	1878.48
	Share of interregional TiVA in interregional trade (%)								
Northeast		55.58	59.27	62.79	56.93	73.33	72.51	79.19	63.57
North Munici-palities	43.69		45.51	35.22	22.40	55.39	56.91	69.65	45.32
North Coast	67.08	48.35		50.48	51.22	63.76	68.29	93.60	56.21
East Coast	64.13	55.75	56.41		39.48	52.68	67.64	79.71	54.95
South Coast	48.87	44.93	51.68	36.11		51.28	53.16	55.09	49.21
Central	78.76	69.04	58.13	56.14	51.64		77.90	88.13	62.84
Northwest	63.29	59.72	60.21	49.12	51.58	66.23		71.33	60.45
Southwest	77.11	75.94	76.30	65.39	51.23	83.67	74.03		69.23
Total	63.30	54.74	55.62	50.32	46.36	57.77	67.56	69.64	57.21

(*Continued*)

Table 7.3. (*Continued*)

	NE	NM	NC	EC	SC	CE	NW	SW	Total
				2007					

	NE	NM	NC	EC	SC	CE	NW	SW	Total
Interregional trade (billion Chinese yuan, current price)									
Northeast		156.63	255.09	205.34	172.34	243.57	97.56	115.55	1246.08
North Municipality	120.93		726.21	137.79	101.07	199.30	94.87	84.18	1464.35
North Coast	123.90	418.62		265.45	203.99	624.79	205.53	125.58	1967.86
East Coast	57.09	62.86	187.70		609.47	681.43	116.56	119.56	1834.67
South Coast	167.18	98.36	192.61	335.80		557.84	235.70	604.27	2191.76
Central	61.70	75.45	463.24	910.49	424.85		153.04	136.09	2224.86
Northwest	84.49	86.32	283.05	318.80	209.95	411.93		230.23	1624.77
Southwest	57.53	27.75	100.20	159.94	335.55	247.54	154.42		1082.93
Total	672.82	925.99	2208.10	2333.61	2057.22	2966.40	1057.68	1415.46	13637.28
Interregional TiVA (billion Chinese yuan, current price)									
Northeast		55.83	125.98	101.49	75.94	149.39	47.57	69.01	625.21
North Municipalities	50.92		328.30	63.81	42.80	122.99	43.46	57.66	709.94
North Coast	59.48	118.25		129.48	88.19	314.48	79.02	91.36	880.26
East Coast	31.69	20.58	83.60		159.34	274.31	48.95	79.01	697.48
South Coast	65.52	25.65	78.29	108.22		237.88	82.04	244.63	842.23
Central	41.45	37.92	182.42	381.08	145.26		67.69	98.07	953.89
Northwest	43.99	37.20	144.55	155.51	90.13	238.89		139.35	849.62
Southwest	35.31	16.26	58.82	82.46	125.50	163.93	75.10		557.38
Total	328.36	311.69	1001.96	1022.05	727.16	1501.87	443.83	779.09	6116.01
Share of interregional TiVA in interregional trade (%)									
Northeast		35.64	49.39	49.43	44.06	61.33	48.76	59.72	50.17
North Municipalities	42.11		45.21	46.31	42.35	61.71	45.81	68.50	48.48
North Coast	48.01	28.25		48.78	43.23	50.33	38.45	72.75	44.73
East Coast	55.51	32.74	44.54		26.14	40.26	42.00	66.08	38.02
South Coast	39.19	26.08	40.65	32.23		42.64	34.81	40.48	38.43
Central	67.18	50.26	39.38	41.85	34.19		44.23	72.06	42.87
Northwest	52.07	43.10	51.07	48.78	42.93	57.99		60.53	52.29
Southwest	61.38	58.59	58.70	51.56	37.40	66.22	48.63		51.47
Total	48.80	33.66	45.38	43.80	35.35	50.63	41.96	55.04	44.85

Source: Author's own calculations.

7.4.4. *Evolution of regional comparative advantage in terms of domestic trade in value added*

There is no guarantee that providing more products equals gaining more value added in a supply chain with high vertical specialization, as in the case of the iPhone. This becomes crucial when considering regional comparative advantage from the view of value creation within the domestic market. This is why we propose to use the TiVA concept to measure regional comparative advantage.

Table 7.4 shows TiVA-based domestic RCA indicator and its changing pattern between 2002 and 2007. The main findings can be summarized as follows: First, there is a large variation of RCA by sector across regions. Namely, the coastal regions have relatively more sectors with top ranking RCA, especially in the manufacturing sector, while the inland regions mainly specialize in primary sectors. Second, the ranking of a region in RCA by sector changes significantly between 2002 and 2007. For example, in 2002, the northeast ranks first for metal products, but in 2007 the central region has taken over the top position. This is mainly because the central region has experienced rapid development of manufacturing sector, especially for metal products compared to other sectors in the same region over the 5-year period. And third, most regions tend to enhance their industrial specialization in value creation when taking part in DVCs, as shown by positive rates of change of standard deviation of RCA by sector.

7.4.5. *Participation degree of regional economy in global markets*

As shown in equation (7.6), using the interregional I/O framework we can also estimate how much of a region's value added is created by another region's exports. This can help us understand the position of a specific region in another region's supply chains.

Figure 7.3 shows the gain potential of induced value added by regional exports. We see that the central region, with its large economy and centralized location, maintains the position as the largest beneficiary of value added spillover from other regions' exports for both 2002 and 2007. Looking at the components of the bars in 2002, exports of the south coast had the largest impact on the value creation of other regions, followed by the east

Table 7.4. Trade in value added-based domestic revealed comparative advantage indicator and its changing pattern, 2002 and 2007.

	Agriculture	Mining and quarrying	Food products and tobacco	Textile and garment	Wood products and furniture	Pulp, paper, and printing	Chemical	Non-metallic mineral products	Metal products	General machinery	Transport equipment	Electric appliances and electronics	Other manufacturing products	Electricity, gas, and water supply	Construction	Trade and transportation	Other services
2002																	
Northeast	0.55	1.74	0.50	0.14	0.53	0.26	1.60	0.07	1.26	1.02	2.14	0.35	0.61	0.82	0.40	1.14	0.96
North Municipalities	0.10	0.52	0.24	0.18	0.14	0.40	0.65	0.32	0.49	0.70	0.79	2.45	0.66	0.43	1.90	0.62	3.02
North Coast	1.39	1.00	2.00	1.52	0.27	1.54	0.97	2.15	0.98	1.30	0.34	0.29	0.81	1.01	0.36	0.96	0.55
East Coast	0.46	0.12	0.47	2.14	0.46	1.20	1.38	0.39	1.08	1.71	1.09	1.25	1.26	0.76	1.56	1.01	1.36
South Coast	0.74	0.72	0.73	0.81	2.36	1.40	0.87	0.32	0.74	0.65	1.50	2.66	2.04	0.73	0.30	1.32	0.87
Central	1.65	1.39	1.00	0.90	1.33	0.68	0.80	1.89	1.11	0.86	0.75	0.38	0.77	1.17	0.31	0.95	0.65
Northwest	1.27	2.68	0.61	0.24	0.26	0.42	0.76	0.82	0.86	0.26	0.41	0.30	0.29	1.24	3.92	0.84	0.99
Southwest	1.47	0.95	2.44	0.34	1.50	1.37	0.66	1.57	1.15	0.65	0.72	0.27	0.55	1.83	1.23	0.82	0.65
SD	0.53	0.75	0.74	0.68	0.74	0.49	0.33	0.76	0.24	0.42	0.56	0.95	0.51	0.40	1.17	0.20	0.75

(*Continued*)

Table 7.4. (Continued)

	Agriculture	Mining and quarrying	Food products and tobacco	Textile and garment	Wood products and furniture	Pulp, paper, and printing	Chemical	Non-metallic mineral products	Metal products	General machinery	Transport equipment	Electric appliances and electronics	Other manufacturing products	Electricity, gas, and water supply	Construction	Trade and transportation	Other services
Northeast	1.45	2.19	1.00	0.05	1.00	0.36	1.68	0.71	0.69	0.62	3.07	0.20	0.64	1.20	1.51	0.68	0.39
North Municipalities	0.12	0.42	0.51	0.09	0.06	0.30	0.57	0.15	0.38	0.63	0.99	0.49	0.80	0.54	0.31	0.96	3.01
North Coast	1.30	0.97	1.00	0.93	2.24	0.99	1.09	2.03	1.27	0.74	0.68	0.40	0.54	0.71	0.02	0.87	1.04
East Coast	0.24	0.10	0.43	1.20	0.30	1.06	1.83	0.40	0.96	2.24	1.51	2.75	2.09	0.64	0.66	1.09	1.01
South Coast	0.32	0.28	0.19	4.35	2.12	2.98	0.66	1.01	1.03	2.61	0.40	2.70	2.18	1.16	0.21	0.92	0.66
Central	1.44	1.09	1.19	0.47	1.07	1.07	1.03	1.73	1.41	0.59	0.50	0.81	0.90	1.05	0.79	1.19	0.58
Northwest	1.43	2.28	1.31	0.22	0.18	0.31	0.65	0.66	0.75	0.17	0.35	0.19	0.16	1.24	2.02	1.09	0.87
Southwest	1.71	0.56	2.76	0.10	0.55	0.50	0.58	0.78	1.40	0.28	1.32	0.29	0.67	1.59	3.26	1.16	0.49
SD	0.61	0.78	0.74	1.35	0.79	0.83	0.47	0.60	0.34	0.86	0.84	1.03	0.69	0.33	1.03	0.16	0.79
Change rate of SD (%)	16	5	0	100	7	70	44	−21	46	104	50	8	35	−16	−12	−19	5

*SD: Standard Deviation ▮ : first rank ▮ : second rank.

Source: Author's own calculations.

2007

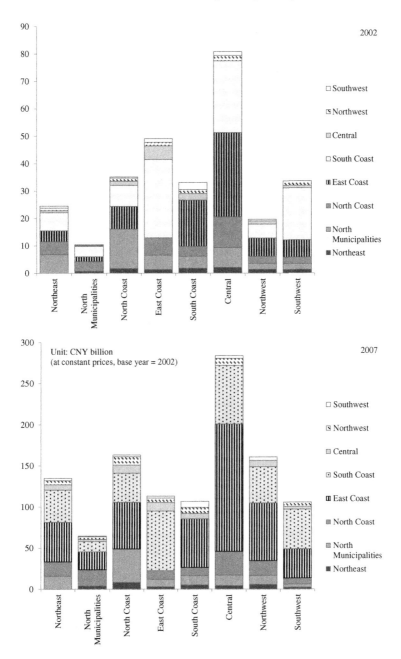

Figure 7.3. Gain potential of induced value added by regional exports, 2002 and 2007.
Source: Author's own calculations.

coast. However, in 2007, the east coast replaced the south coast's position and became the most important driving force to create other regions' value added. In addition, looking at the evolution of inland regions, it is easy to see that more inland regions enjoy the benefits from their partner region's exports, especially from the south coast and east coast. Taken together, this means that the inland regions in the PRC have been increasing their participation in the GVCs by exporting more products to the world market directly, but also indirectly by joining the domestic supply chains of leading coastal regions.

7.5. Conclusion

The PRC has experienced rapid economic growth since the launch of the Reform and Open-Door Policy in 1978. With the accession to the WTO in 2001, the PRC has become deeply involved in the world economy. The PRC's participation in global supply chains has had dramatic impacts not only on its domestic economy but also the global trade structure. To elucidate the increasing complexity of the PRC's domestic production networks, this chapter focused on the measure of DVCs across regions and their linkages with global markets. Using the PRC's 2002 and 2007 interregional input–output tables, this chapter measured detailed structural changes in domestic TiVA, and the position and degree of participation of different regions in both DVCs and GVCs.

The main conclusions can be summarized as follows: First, the creation and distribution of value added across regions has become more flat. This is primarily due to the expansion of interregional trade with high vertical specialization trade in intermediate products. Second, the final demand for goods and services produced in other regions has played a large role in the development of trans-regional value added trade. Third, most of the inland regions successfully enhanced their gain potential for value added by increasing their participation in DVCs. Fourth, the PRC's increased participation in GVCs between 2002 and 2007 can be mainly attributed to the increasing presence of inland regions in the production chains. Fifth, the inland regions were able to get much more value added not only by increasing direct exports to the world market, but also by joining the domestic supply chains of leading coastal regions. And last, regional TiVA-based comparative advantages across sectors show a more apparent tendency toward concentration. This indirectly reflects the improved efficiency of the PRC's DVCs.

Appendix 7A. Regional Classification of the People's Republic of China.

Regions (8)	Provincial level divisions (31)
Northeast	Liaoning (6), Jilin (7), Heilongjiang (8)
North Municipalities	Beijing (1), Tianjin (2)
North Coast	Hebei (3), Shandong (15)
East Coast	Shanghai (9), Jiangsu (10), Zhejiang (11)
South Coast	Fujian (13), Guangdong (19), Hainan (21)
Central	Shanxi (4), Anhui (12), Jiangxi (14), Henan (16), Hubei (17), Hunan (18)
Northwest	Inner Mongolia Autonomous Region (5), Shaanxi (27), Gansu (28), Qinghai (29), Ningxia Hui Autonomous Region (30), Xinjiang Uyghur Autonomous Region (31)
Southwest	Guangxi Zhuang Autonomous Region (20), Chongqing (22), Sichuan (23), Guizhou (24), Yunnan (25), Tibet Autonomous Region (26)

References*

Balassa, B. 1965. Trade Liberalization and Revealed Comparative Advantage. *The Manchester School* 33(2): 99–123.

Dedrick, J., K.L. Kraemer, and G. Linden. 2010. Who Profits from Innovation in Global Value Chains? A Study of the iPod and Notebook PCs. *Industrial and Corporate Change* 19(1): 81–116.

Degain, C. and A. Maurer. 2010. Globalization and Trade Flows: What You See Is Not What You Get! WTO Staff Working Paper.

Escaith, H. 2008. Measuring Trade in Value Added in the New Industrial Economy: Statistical Implications. MPRA Paper No. 14454.

---

*The Asian Development Bank refers to China by the name People's Republic of China.

Fukasaku, K., B. Meng, and N. Yamano. 2011. Recent Development in Asian Economic Integration: Measuring Trade Integration and Fragmentation. OECD STI Working Paper, 2011/3.

Hioki, S., G.J.D. Hewings, and N. Okamoto. 2009 Identifying the Structural Changes of China's Spatial Production Linkages Using a Qualitative Input–Output Analysis. *The Journal of Econometric Study of Northeast Asia* 6(2): 25–55.

Hummels, D., J. Ishii, and K.M. Yi. 2001. The Nature and Growth of Vertical Specialization in World Trade. *Journal of International Economics* 54(1): 75–96.

Johnson, R.C. and G. Noguera. 2011. Accounting for Intermediates: Production Sharing and Trade in Value Added. *Journal of International Economics* 86(2): 224–236.

Kuroiwa, I. 2006. Rules of Origin and Local Content in East Asia. IDE Discussion Paper No. 78, IDE-JETRO.

Koopman, R., Z. Wang, and S.J. Wei. 2008. How Much of Chinese Exports Is Really Made in China? Assessing Domestic Value Added When Processing Trade Is Pervasive. NBER Working Paper No. 14109.

Koopman, R., W. Powers, Z. Wang, and S.J. Wei. 2010. Give Credit Where Credit is Due: Tracing Value Added in Global Production Chains. NBER Working Paper No. 16426.

Linden, G., J. Dedrick, and K.L. Kraemer. 2009. Innovation and Job Creation in a Global Economy: The Case of Apple's iPod. Working Paper, Personal Computing Industry Center, UC Irvine.

Los, B., E. Dietzenbacher, R. Stehrer, M.P. Timmer, and G. de Vries. 2012. Trade Performance in Internationally Fragmented Production Networks: Concepts and Measures. WIOD Working Paper, 11.

Meng, B. and C. Qu. 2008. Application of the Input–Output Decomposition Technique to China's Regional Economies. *Journal of Applied Regional Science* 13: 27–46.

Meng, B., N. Yamano, and C. Webb. 2010. Application of Factor Decomposition Techniques to Vertical Specialisation Measurements. *Journal of Applied Input–Output Analysis* 16: 1–20.

Meng, B., Y. Fang, and N. Yamano. 2012. Measuring Global Value Chains and Regional Economic Integration: An International Input–Output Approach. IDE Discussion Paper No. 362, IDE-JETRO.

Pei, J., J. Oosterhaven, and E. Dietzenbacher. 2012. International Trade, Spillovers and Regional Income Disparity. ARTNeT/WTO Research Workshop on Emerging Trade Issues in Asia and the Pacific: Meeting Contemporary Policy Challenges 2012.

Stehrer, R. 2012. Trade in Value Added and Value Added in Trade. WIIW Working Paper No. 81.

Timmer, M.P., B. Los, R. Stehrer, and G.J. de Vries. 2013. Fragmentation, Incomes and Jobs: An Analysis of European Competitiveness. *Economic Policy*, October: 615–660.

Uchida, Y. and S. Inomata. 2009. Vertical Specialization in the Time of the Economic Crisis. In *Asia Beyond the Global Economic Crisis: The Transmission Mechanism of Financial Shocks: The Transmission Mechanism of Financial Shocks*, edited by S. Inomata and Y. Uchida. Cheltenham, UK: Edward Elgar.

Xing, Y. and N. Detert. 2010. How the iPhone Widens the United States Trade Deficit with the People's Republic of China. ADBI Working Paper No. 257. Tokyo: Asian Development Bank Institute.

Yang, C.H., E. Dietzenbacher, J.S. Pei, and X.K. Chen. 2009. The Bias in Measuring Vertical Specialization. Paper presented at the 17th International Input–Output Association Conference.

Zhang, Y.X. and S.C. Qi. 2012. *China's Interregional Input–Output Tables for 2002 and 2007*. China Statistics Press (in Chinese).

Zhang, Y.X. and K. Zhao. 2004. The Spillover and Feedback Effects between Coastal and Non-Coastal Regions. In *Spatial Structure and Regional Development in China: Interregional Input–Output Approach*, edited by N. Okamoto and T. Ihara. Basingstoke: Palgrave Macmillan, IDE-JETRO Series.

Chapter 8

The "Fox–Apple" Partnership in the Global Value Chain: How Did Foreign Direct Investment and Contract Manufacturing Reshape the Landscape of the Electronics Industry?

*Guoyong Liang**

Mirroring the notion of Wintel, we have coined the term *Fox–Apple* to describe the "alliance" between Foxconn Technology Group, a contract manufacturer headquartered in Taipei,China, and Apple Inc., an American technology company. Within the global electronics industry, the relationship between these two companies is so important that its formation has reshaped the landscape of the industry over the past decade. This relationship is also very typical in the sense that it reflects the characteristics of an emerging new global value chain in electronics. By examining the emergence and expansion of the *Fox–Apple* partnership, this chapter tries to explore the latest pattern of global production and shed light on the following two questions: What are the new, salient features of global production networks? How have foreign direct investment (FDI) and other modes of multinational companies' international operation (particularly contract manufacturing) led to these features? It proposes a theoretical hypothesis based on ownership, location, and externalization (OLE) advantages for understanding firms' strategic choice between FDI and international outsourcing.

8.1. Introduction

In this chapter, we use the term *Fox–Apple* to describe the particular relationship between two companies.[1] Apple Inc., headquartered in Silicon Valley in the United States (US), is a leading company in the global

---

*The views expressed in this paper are those of the author only and do not necessarily represent those of the United Nations.

[1]The author first introduced the concept of "Fox–Apple" in an article in Chinese published in "Southern Metropolitan News," a newspaper in the PRC, on 7 November 2012. Research for this chapter was undertaken in 2012, and all data contained in the text, tables, and figures of the chapter reflect the situation as of that year.

electronics industry, with annual sales of over US$100 billion, quarterly profits of nearly US$10 billion, and a market capitalization reaching a level of above US$600 billion.[2] Foxconn Technology Group, with its parent company Hon Hai Precision Industry headquartered in Taipei,China, is the dominant player in electronics manufacturing, employing more than 1 million workers in the People's Republic of China (PRC) and generating annual sales of US$100 billion and a combined import and export volume of over US$200 billion a year. The size of the two companies shows the significance of the partnership: The US brand owner and the PRC contract manufacturer ranked 55th and 43th, respectively, in the 2012 Fortune Global 500 List.

Our creation of the concept *Fox–Apple* was inspired by that of *Wintel*, which appeared about two decades ago for describing the alliance between Microsoft and Intel. We have coined the term *Fox–Apple* because it captures the specific "symbiotic" relation between Apple Inc. and Foxconn Technology, as well as its importance in the global electronics industry. Like the creation of the *Wintel* partnership, which used to dominate the evolution of the world's information technology (IT) industry in the 1980s and the 1990s, the formation of the *Fox–Apple* partnership has reshaped the landscape of this industry since the mid-2010s.

As a technological revolution took place in the IT industry in the early 1980s, Intel and Microsoft established a strategic partnership based on the core product of the industry: the personal computer (PC). The former dominated the production of the principal hardware of PCs — the central processing unit (CPU) — while the latter monopolized the most important software — operating system — and extended its market dominance to other software products. Since then, the PC has remained the key product in the electronics and IT industry, and the *Wintel* partnership has experienced an enduring dominance in the PC segment of the industry. In the early- and mid-2000s, however, a new round of technological

---

[2]Revenues of Apple Inc. amounted to US$108 billion in 2011. Its quarterly revenues were US$36 billion in the fourth quarter of 2012, with a net profit of US$8 billion. The company's share price reached US$700 in September 2012, making the capitalization of the company at a historical high of about US$660 billion. The share price of Apple has substantially declined since.

revolution took place, as various new products such as advanced digital devices and smartphones emerged based on the convergence of digital consumer electronics, mobile telecommunications, and PC technologies, as well as on technological advances related to major electronics components.[3] During this critical process of technological and industrial transformation, Apple has successfully introduced its "killer products" and quickly emerged as the major winner, leaving traditional makers of PCs and mobile phones behind in the market competition. Its success has been to a large extent based on the support of Foxconn, as well as from a large number of component suppliers.

The formation of the *Wintel* was around the product, while that of *Fox–Apple* is along the value chain. Global value chains (GVCs) in the electronics industry emerged in the late 1980s and early 1990s as outsourcing of production processes started to take place in a significant manner. Since then, electronics GVCs have been rapidly expanding, as reflected by the fragmentation of production processes, the delocalization of economic activities, and the division of labor between different types of enterprises, as well as their clear-cut positioning in different stages of the value chain. Brand owners, mostly based in industrial countries, focus on product development and marketing, while contract manufacturers, mostly based in emerging economies, concentrate on supply chain management, parts procurement, and final assembly. The contract manufacturing model has become standard practice in many segments in the global IT and electronics industry, including that of the PC.

From *Wintel* to *Fox–Apple*, the global electronics industry has experienced constant and considerable changes, as new technologies, new products, new players, and new winners who "take all" have emerged. A crucial source of dynamism in the industry is in the way the firms' supply chain is organized. Indeed, the industry already experienced a sea change when widespread production offshoring took place in the 1990s and 2000s. In the past decade or so, with the acceleration of technological advances

---

[3]These technological advances are related to various components, such as application processors, flash memory, thin film transistor (TFT) liquid crystal display (LCD), and touch screens. For instance, TFT LCD uses TFT technology to improve image quality such as addressability and contrast.

and introduction of new, sophisticated products, such as smartphones and tablets, the complexity of global value chains in the electronics industries has reached an unprecedented level. This has been partly driven by the expansion of the *Fox–Apple* alliance, in which Apple and Foxconn have established a "win–win" relationship based on close collaboration and mutual dependence. Together they have brought the contract manufacturing model in electronics to a new height.

A number of important questions have emerged with regard to the *Fox–Apple* partnership and the global, national, and industrial contexts of its emergence. How has the strategic partnership between Apple and Foxconn formed and evolved? What is special about the relationship between the two companies compared with a normal "buyer–supplier" relationship in the GVC in electronics? To what extent has the *Fox–Apple* partnership led to the emergence of new, salient features of the GVC, and what are they? What are the technological and institutional drivers of such changes, and what has been the specific role of various modes of multinational companies' (MNCs) international operation, particularly foreign direct investment (FDI) and contract manufacturing? Answers to these questions are crucial for understanding the dynamics in the global electronics industry and their consequences, especially with regard to the value distribution along the chain and between different locations and stakeholders.

From emergence to dominance, the *Apple–Foxconn* alliance has reshaped the landscape of the global electronics industry in less than a decade. By investigating the initial formation and gradual evolution of this partnership, we try to shed light on the above questions, which are of both practical and theoretical relevance. We also discuss the implications for development policy making, especially at the industry level. The starting point of our analysis is inter-firm relationship, which is in line with the traditional GVC approach that links the concept of value added chain with the global organization of industries, and emphasizes the importance of coordination across firm borders.[4] The focus of the analysis is the production stage of the GVC, or the global production network.

---

[4]See Porter (1985) for the concept of "value chain," Davis (1993) for "supply chain management," and Gereffi and Korzeniewicz (1994) for the early literature on the GVC or global commodity chains.

The remaining part of the chapter is organized as follows. The next section provides a narrative of the emergence and evolution of the *Fox–Apple* partnership, analyzes the latest dynamics of the related production network, and summarizes new features of the electronics GVCs. Using *Fox–Apple* as an illustrative case, Section 8.3 explores the determinants of the international outsourcing (subcontracting) model, as well as the complementary role of FDI. It presents a theoretical hypothesis based on ownership, location, and externalization (OLE) advantages. This is followed by a brief discussion in Section 8.4 on the latest tendencies, challenges, and their development implications. The final section concludes.

8.2. *Fox–Apple* and the Global Value Chain

The tale of two firms takes place in the global electronics industry, which is the single most important manufacturing sector in the global economy in terms of both value creation and employment generation, as well as a "propulsive sector" that enhances productivity in other sectors and lowers transaction cost in the economy as a whole. The global electronics industry is highly internationalized, driven by the rapid pace of innovation, proactive internationalization strategy of firms, and generally open and supportive government policies. Widespread production offshoring has taken place, and most advanced GVCs have developed in the industry. As measured by trade in intermediate goods, indeed, GVC formation is most significant in the electronics industry and has experienced the fastest growth since the late 1980s (Sturgeon and Kawakami 2010).

8.2.1. *Global value chain formation in electronics:*
The technological and institutional drivers

The formation of GVCs has been driven by technological progress. The advancement of "general purpose technologies," such as transportation and telecommunications, has shortened the "distance" between countries, and thus promoted international expansion of firms' business operations and facilitated delocalization of the value chain. Furthermore, modularization as well as other advances in production techniques have made subcontracting and outsourcing of production activities increasingly feasible and manageable, and therefore enhanced fragmentation of the value chain. In the electronics and IT industry, in particular, advances in integrated circuits has propelled rapid product and production innovation — as predicted by Moore's Law, the number of transistors increases constantly, which leads to decreased cost and increased functionality, providing a basic source of dynamism in a highly active GVC.

Institutional factors are equally important. After the end of the Cold War in the late 1980s, the world economy entered an era of "strong globalization."[5] Market competition has been largely extended and intensified internationally. More importantly, neoliberal economic thinking and related policy practices have provided a fertile ground for the growth of GVCs. A welcoming investment policy became the dominant practice of most developing countries and made it possible for widespread FDI flows and production relocation from developed to developing countries, which aimed at reducing cost and enhancing efficiency. In the meantime, an increasingly open trade policy regime (as highlighted by the WTO accession of developing economies, especially that of the PRC in 2001) has reduced the cost of imports and exports as well as contributed to an instrumental institutional environment for MNCs' international sourcing practices and supply chain management.

8.2.2. Fox–Apple: *From emergence to dominance*

In a wide range of industries, such as garments and automotives, companies have leveraged technological and institutional change since the late 1980s and significantly extended their supply chains abroad. It is in the electronics industry that the most sophisticated GVC has taken shape. The *Fox–Apple* partnership, its emergence and expansion, has been at the center of the GVC formation in the electronics industry during the past decade.

Since the early-2000s, advanced digital devices (as an extension of consumer electronic devices), smartphones (as an extension of mobile phones), and tablets (as an extension of PCs) have gradually emerged as key products in the electronics and IT industry, with Apple being one main leaders of this revolutionary process of product innovation. Incorporated in

---

[5]The era of "strong globalization" ended in 2008 when the global financial crisis took place. Globalization continues, but at a slower pace, and de-globalization forces, such as protectionist policy measures in trade and investment areas, have gained strength.

1976, Apple experienced a major success in the newborn PC industry in the 1980s, but declined in the 1990s. In 2001, the company reported total sales of US$5.4 billion and an operating loss of 6% of its turnover. In an effort to introduce a consumer digital device to diversify and boost growth, the company launched the iPod (the personal digital music device) in November that year. The product turned out to be a phenomenal success — about 100 million units were sold in the subsequent five years. Apple gradually released other gadgets: iPhone (smartphone) in June 2007, iPod Touch (personal media player and assistant) in September 2007, iPad (tablet computer) in April 2010, and iPad Mini in October 2012. The introduction of these products and continuous upgrade of their models, coupled with Apple's brand and design advantages, have boosted strong market demand and turned Apple into a money-making machine.

Apple's supply chain has been constantly evolving, but the final assembly has been mostly done in the PRC by contract manufacturers from Taipei,China. From the iPod to the iPad, Foxconn has been intensively involved in the production of these new products. Though different models and various generations have been introduced, the production of the iPod has been undertaken primarily by three companies: Inventec Appliances (assembling iPod Classic), Asustek Computer (iPod Mini), and Foxconn (iPod Nano and iPod Shuffle). Foxconn began production of the iPod in 2005, later than Inventec and Asustek, but rapidly gained a monopolistic position in assembling the latest models of the iPod Nano and Shuffle. In 2005, iPod production contributed to about 5% of its total sales of US$23 billion.[6] In 2006, iPod production built up very rapidly at Foxconn's plant in Shenzhen, which at that time already housed more than 200,000 workers.[7] Based on its successful performance in producing the iPad, Foxconn quickly established a dominant position in the production for Apple's other new products — the iPhone and the iPad. In order to keep up with booming demand of the new Apple products, Foxconn expanded its major production base to dozens of locations in the PRC, including large inland cities,

---

[6]In the same year, the production of the iPod contributed to about 60% of Inventec's total sales of US$3.6 billion (Einhorn 2007).
[7]The plant in Shenzhen, near Hong Kong, China produced the iPod Nano, while another one in Suzhou, near Shanghai, produced the iPod Shuffle.

such as Chengdu, Chongqing, Nanning, and Zhengzhou. Accordingly, total employment in the country has surpassed 1.4 million, making Foxconn one of the largest employers in the world.

Foxconn has not only contributed to, but also benefited from, the commercial success of Apple. By 2005, Foxconn had already become the largest contract manufacturer in the world. However, it was its expanding cooperation with Apple that led to its dominant position in contract manufacturing. During 2005–2012, its sales increased fivefold, jumping from US$23 billion to US$118 billion. Currently, Foxconn provides electronics manufacturing services (EMS), including original equipment manufacturing (OEM) and original design manufacturing (ODM), to almost all important brands in computers, communications, and consumer electronics. However, for Foxconn, Apple is the leading customer and its orders account for at least two-thirds of Foxconn's total revenues.[8] Booming demand from Apple has, to a very large extent, boosted sales of Foxconn, resulting in phenomenal growth of the company after the mid-2000s.

For Apple, the partnership with Foxconn has been equally, if not more, important. Apple has been long pursuing a business strategy based on highly innovative technology, high-end products, and high-speed product life cycles. This overall business strategy calls for a manufacturing strategy that puts great emphasis on efficiency (low cost), reliability (high quality), and flexibility (quick reaction and adjustment). In the 1980s, Apple produced its main products, PCs, by itself in locations such as Fremont, California and Fountain, Colorado in the US. Since the early 1990s, the company increasingly located its PC production abroad, especially in Asia, which reflected an overall trend in electronics in general and the PC industry in particular at the time.[9] Since the early 2000s, Apple introduced its "gadgets" and resorted to contract manufacturing from the beginning in search for

---

[8]No accurate information exists concerning the extent to which the business relationship with Apple contributes to Foxconn's total sales and profits. Our estimation is based on the consideration of the following factors: (i) Apple's total sales in 2011, (ii) Apple's sales that can be attributed to the iPod, iPhone, and iPad, the assembly of which have been primarily done by Foxconn, and (iii) Foxconn's total sales in 2011.

[9]By mid-2000s, Quanta, Compal, Wistron, Inventec, and Asustek, all from Taipei,China, had dominated the OEM and ODM businesses for PCs, and the production network had concentrated in the PRC (Foster *et al.* 2006).

higher efficiency and greater flexibility. Apple did not start with Foxconn right away, but orders concentrated gradually to the latter as a result of its "total cost" solutions and advantages, its proprietary eCMMS (Electronic Component Module Move and Service) model, and its high capability, flexibility, and reliability. That unique flexibility, including the ability to respond to specific requirements and adjust the scale and specification of production quickly, seems to be one of the main reasons that Apple has outsourced its production to Asia, and mostly to Foxconn.[10]

Apart from the *Fox–Apple* partnership, the core part of the GVC, a large number of component producers/suppliers are associated with the production of the iPod, the iPhone, and the iPad.[11] In total, more than 150 companies are involved as suppliers in 2012, but only a relatively limited number of large companies are responsible for the production and supply of important, high-value components (Table 8.1). Sometimes a set of smaller companies providing subcomponents are involved, with the major component supplier being an integrator/assembler and coordinating its own supply chain. This multi-layer, multi-faceted, and multi-location network of firms makes up a production network that reflects the growing complexity of the global electronics GVCs. Though Apple may have a contractual relationship with many of the suppliers, the daily logistical and operational interactions are mostly with Foxconn.

The *Fox–Apple* partnership goes well beyond a conventional relationship between supplier and buyer, and involves intensive and extensive collaboration between Apple and Foxconn at various levels: From daily business function to strategic decision-making. Considered mutually dependent and beneficial, the partnership represents a symbiotic and win–win inter-firm relationship. For either Apple or Foxconn, its business success cannot be achieved without the other. The relationship seems to be quite stable, possibly as a result of mutual trust and satisfaction, and possibly due to the fact that an alternative partner does not exist, at least until now.

---

[10]See, for instance, Duhigg and Bradsher (2012).
[11]A total of 156 companies are included in the supplier list published for the first time by Apple in 2012. It is unclear how many of them are for the production of the iPod, iPhone, and iPad, respectively.

Table 8.1. Main components of Apple's new products and major producers.

Product	Key component[d]	Major producer	Location[e]
iPod[a]	Hard drive	Toshiba	Japan
	Display module	Toshiba-Matsushita	Japan
	Application processor	Broadcom	United States
	Portal Player CPU	Portal Player	United States
	Display Driver	Renesas	Japan
	SDRAM-Mobile memory	Samsung Electronics	Republic of Korea
	...		
iPhone[b]	Flash memory	Toshiba	Japan
	Display module	Toshiba	Japan
	Touch screen	Toshiba	Japan
	Application processor	Samsung Electronics	Republic of Korea
	SDRAM-Mobile DDR	Samsung Electronics	Republic of Korea
	Baseband	Infineon	Germany
	Camera Module	Infineon	Germany
	RF Transceiver	Infineon	Germany
	GPS Receiver	Infineon	Germany
	Bluetooth/WLAN/FM	Broadcom	United States
	MCP Memory	Numonyx	United States
	...		
iPad[c]	Display module	LG Electronics	Republic of Korea
	Multi-touch screen	Wintek	Taipei,China
	NAND flash memory	Toshiba/Samsung	Japan/Republic of Korea
	Lithium polymer battery	Amperex Technology	Hong Kong, China
	A4 processor	Samsung Electronics	Republic of Korea
	MCP Memory	Samsung Electronics	Republic of Korea
	Bluetooth/WLAN/FM	Broadcom	United States
	...		

Notes:
[a]The fifth generation of iPod Classic released in October 2005.
[b]iPhone 3G released in July 2008.
[c]The first generation of iPad released in April 2010.
[d]Ranked according to the estimated cost.
[e]The location where the ultimate parent company is located.
Source: Linden *et al.* (2007), Xing and Detert (2010), iSuppli, and author's own research.

From a broader perspective, a large number of inter-firm relations (related to different brands and products) exist in the global electronics industry. Among all the pairs, that between Apple and Foxconn is (i) the largest in terms of the size of the two companies and their commercial exchanges, (ii) the most significant in terms of its industrial and economic influence, and (iii) perhaps a dominant one as reflected by the competitive positions of both companies in their respective industries and along different lines of products. Against the background of a period of strong globalization, *Fox–Apple* has become the largest "fruit" on the tree of GVCs: from emergence to dominance, it has reshaped the landscape of the global electronics industry in a period of less than a decade.

8.3. New Global Value Chains: Features and Implications

The globally disbursed, highly integrated production networks, as high-lighted by the *Fox–Apple* partnership, have emerged in a number of important segments of the electronics industry, involving both end products and components. Similar relations exist between firms in the value chains of many products, but on a smaller scale and with less significance. What is different in the segments of new products of advanced digital devices, smartphones, and tablets, where the *Fox–Apple* story took place, is that the production pattern is "born global"[12]: An evolutionary process from vertical integration, to domestic subcontracting, and then to international outsourcing (or production offshoring) did not take place; rather, production was outsourced to foreign contract manufacturers right from the beginning.

The evolution of the *Fox–Apple* partnership illustrates some new patterns in the electronics GVC. First, a new type of "buyer–supplier" relationship with distinctive characteristics has emerged. This is a partnership between two leading firms at two key stages of the value chain. Within the inter-firm relationship, Foxconn as the supplier has a relatively high degree of power *vis-à-vis* Apple as the buyer. This may be from its size (Foxconn is even larger than Apple in terms of sales), its knowledge and ownership advantages (in terms of process innovation, low-cost production, and efficient management), and the high concentration of orders from Apple. The dependence *vice versa* exists, perhaps related to the heavy reliance on one firm for production. This new power relationship along the value chain is different from both the traditional producer- and buyer-driven

---

[12]The term "born global" is borrowed from the literature on the internationalization strategy of firms (for example, see Knight 1997).

models in the early analysis of GVC governance (Gereffi 1999). It seems to represent a hybrid form of modular, relational, and captive model of governance structures in electronics GVCs (Sturgeon 2002; Gereffi *et al.* 2005). Reflecting the new dynamics within the GVC,[13] this relationship seems to be mutually captive and relatively stable.

Second, GVCs have demonstrated a number of new structural features. The current picture of the electronics industry, particularly segments of new products such as smartphones and tablets, demonstrate that a *new global value chain* is emerging. As illustrated by Apple's supply network, Foxconn as the final assembler coordinates inputs from some key suppliers of major components, while these suppliers often have their own supply chains and receive inputs from smaller component suppliers — a "root" structure exists for the production of the final product (Figure 8.1). In addition, with a strong focus on innovation (both product and process), the core relationship between the brand owner and the final assembler presents the "trunk," while the distribution network seems to be the "crown." Therefore, "global value tree" becomes a term better than "global value chain" in reflecting the new structure of the value creation network. There have been few studies exploring the overall structure of the GVC, and the tree metaphor is an attempt in filling the gap.

Third, new features of the GVCs have important impacts for the global electronics industry. By combining a business strategy based on aggressive product innovation and a supportive manufacturing strategy based on proactive process innovation and extreme efficiency solutions, *Fox–Apple,* the alliance between two leaders in the respective areas, has largely increased the availability of new electronic products, and more importantly enhanced their affordability. As a result, markets have been created by both product innovation of the brand owner and supportive process innovation of contract manufacturer, which have been turned into a phenomenal commercial success along the value chain: from raw material to component and content suppliers to telecom operators and other distributers. A virtuous circle has appeared, which is instrumental to enterprise development and innovation at various levels. Beyond the industrial border, traditional sectors

---

[13]Recent theorizing about the governance of GVCs highlights three key determinants: complexity, codifiability, and supplier competence (Sturgeon and Gereffi 2009).

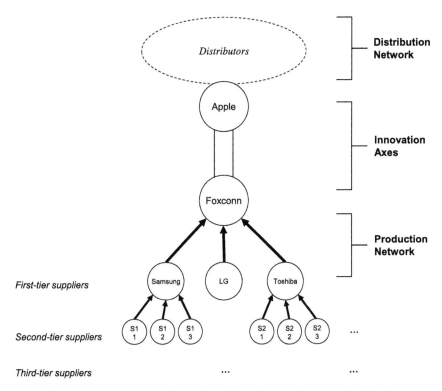

Figure 8.1. A global value tree: Illustration of the value creation network of Apple.

such as entertainment and telecommunications have been strongly affected as well.

Finally, broader economic and social implications of the *new global value chain* deserve particular attention. A number of studies examine value distribution along the value chain: investigative product accounting has been applied to the iPod (Linden *et al.* 2007), the iPhone (Xing and Detert 2010), and the iPad (Kraemer *et al.* 2011), demonstrating how value is shared among companies and countries. The implications for trade flows are so important that trade patterns as predicted by conventional theories are reversed and conventional trade statistics give a misleading picture (Xing and Detert 2010). Following the seminal study on iPhone (Xing and Detert 2010), concepts and methodologies of trade in value added have been introduced (OECD and WTO 2013). Social implications have been discussed as well, with a focus on worker incomes and working conditions in the assembly stage of the value chain.

Empirical examination of the new phenomenon has generated valuable insights on economic impacts of the new features of the GVCs in electronics. However, how such features emerge and lead to the various impacts mentioned above remains unanswered. In addition, deeper insights about consequences on innovation, industrialization, and development are called for. The existing literature on the GVC cannot help us adequately understand the drivers and determinants of the new phenomenon and its broader consequences. The missing links are at firm, product, and plant levels, and a critical research question concerns how foreign direct investment and other modes of multinational companies' international operation (particularly contract manufacturing) have led to the emergence of the new features of the electronics GVCs.

8.4. Foreign Direct Investment, Contract Manufacturing, and the Global Value Chain: *Fox–Apple* as an Illustrative Case

Since the early 1990s, electronics GVCs have been rapidly evolving and expanding, driven by proactive international strategy and operation of MNCs. MNCs' cross-border business practices are complex, including investing, outsourcing, partnering, licensing, franchising, and so on. Among these business activities, FDI and contract manufacturing are the two most important channels through which GVCs are formed. In other words, FDI and contract manufacturing present two basic models in which production offshoring takes place. In the FDI model, MNCs in industrialized countries invest in emerging economies and produce there by themselves. In the contract manufacturing model, MNCs outsource production to contract manufacturers operating in emerging economies. Thus, the interrelationship between the two deserves particular attention in a theoretical endeavor for understanding the new dynamics of production networks.

8.4.1. *Foreign direct investment and international outsourcing: Substitutes or complements?*

Theoretically, a firm faces the following sequence of decisions in organizing the whole process of economic activities, particularly with regard to

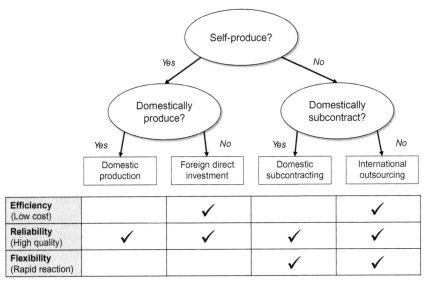

Figure 8.2. Decision-making processes and objectives concerning foreign direct investment and outsourcing.

production: (i) to remain vertically integrated and undertake the job by itself, or to subcontract it to a supplier, (ii) if remaining vertically integrated, to undertake the job domestically or abroad, or (iii) if subcontracting, to outsource it to a domestic supplier, or to a foreign one (Figure 8.2). The first option is the standard "make or buy" question, which dates back to the early emergence of the theory of the firm. However, international dimension of subcontracting makes the issue more complicated. For brand owners in high-income countries, the two basic options — outward FDI and international outsourcing — are likely to be substitutive for reducing cost and enhancing efficiency of production. The current picture of the global electronics industry shows that the second option takes the lead, as international outsourcing has become a dominant means of minimizing operational risks in a dynamic industrial setting, where vertical integration alone does not provide a sustainable competitive advantage.[14]

---

[14]For example, see Curry and Kenney (1999) for a discussion on the issue.

G. Liang

Although both outward FDI and international outsourcing can help Western brand owners leverage favorable production conditions in emerging economies to reduce costs, international outsourcing provides a much greater degree of flexibility, which has become an increasingly important element in the new manufacturing strategy. Particularly for new products such as smartphones and tablets, market demand changes rapidly and product (as well as model) life cycles have been largely shortened. In the face of intensified competition and market volatility, production facilities must be able to do the following adjustments very quickly: (i) to reconfigure for new products; (ii) to increase production from pilot to maximum demand; (iii) to adjust the production scale depending on volatile market demand; and (iv) to be prepared for the end of the product or model life cycle.[15] Facing the choice between managing production by themselves and outsourcing to contract manufacturers, Western brand owners often prefer the latter in order to increase flexibility and reduce risk.

However, the *Fox–Apple* partnership and the related production network have demonstrated the crucial complementary role of FDI for contract manufacturing. The success of contract manufacturing and international outsourcing in electronics is based on two main factors: First, the availability of capable contract manufacturers, which can fulfill the increasingly sophisticated work of supply chain management, parts procurement, and product assembly. Second, the affordability of contract manufacturing services, which requires low cost of production factors (for example labor and land) and high efficiency of contract manufacturing. The two factors have led to a dominant pattern of capable contract manufacturers from high-income countries (including the newly industrialized economies, or NIEs) investing in low-income countries, while serving brand owners based in high-income countries. This pattern has been reinforced by the abundant supply of cheap factors (labor and land), improved infrastructure, and concentrated supply base, especially in a limited number of emerging economies such as the PRC.

---

[15]For example, see Lee (2012) for the discussion of Apple's manufacturing strategy and the requirements for contract manufacturers; Skinner (1969) for an early discussion on the manufacturing strategy of firms.

Historically, the largest contract manufacturers, including Flextronics, Jabil, Sanmina-SCI, and Benchmark Electronics, were based in the US (Sturgeon and Kawakami 2010). However, they have gradually shifted to Asia in order to take advantage of specific production conditions there. For instance, Flextronics was founded in Silicon Valley in 1969. The company relocated its headquarters to Singapore in 1990, closed its plant in the US in 1996, and invested heavily in Asia, including both mergers and acquisitions as well as greenfield investments. It is currently the world's second largest contract manufacturer, only behind Foxconn. Established in 1966, Jabil is still headquartered in the US, but it has expanded its production facilities to a number of Asian countries, such as the PRC, Malaysia, and Viet Nam, and has acquired some Asian companies. Currently, the largest contract manufacturers are mainly based in Asia, with headquarters in the NIEs: Taipei,China; Hong Kong, China; and Singapore. Through FDI, they have located their production facilities in relatively low-income Asian economies, particularly the PRC. In the meantime, they have outperformed traditional Western contract manufacturers and have become a dominant force in the assembly part of the electronics GVCs.

In the production of Apple's new products, contract manufacturers for both the end product and major components are headquartered in high-income economies (including the NIEs). As the final assembler of the product and major coordinator of the value chain, Foxconn has undertaken a huge amount of FDI for producing in the PRC. The major component suppliers, such as Toshiba and Samsung Electronics, produced the high-value components mainly in their home economies, but have relocated part of the production activities to emerging economies, particularly the PRC (Table 8.2). This is partly due to cost considerations, and partly driven by the motive to be closer to important customers for inventory and delivery reasons. For instance, Samsung has stated it will invest in a US$7 billion factory to produce NAND flash memory in Xi'an (Shanxi Province). To be operational at the end of 2013, the plant is Samsung's largest ever overseas investment and will become its second largest memory chip production base in the world. The decision of producing the most advanced and highest value-added components in the PRC has been driven by the fact that the country is now the leading market of these components, fueled by the fast-growing production of new electronics devices such as the iPhone and the iPad.

Table 8.2. Major production locations of Apple's key component suppliers.

Major producer	Key component[a]	Major production locations
Toshiba	Hard drive	PRC
	Display module	Japan (PRC after 2009)
	Touch screen	Japan
	NAND flash memory	Japan
	...	
Samsung Electronics[b]	SDRAM-Mobile memory	Republic of Korea
	Application processor	Republic of Korea, United States
	MCP Memory	Republic of Korea
	NAND flash memory	Republic of Korea (PRC after 2013)
	...	
Broadcom[c]	Application processor	PRC and Taipei,China
	Bluetooth/WLAN/FM	PRC and Taipei,China
	...	
Portal Player	Portal Player CPU	United States and Taipei,China
Renesas	Display Driver	Japan
Infineon	RF systems	Germany[d]
LG Electronics	Display	Republic of Korea
Wintek	Multi-touch screen	PRC; Taipei,China; Viet Nam
Amperex Technology	Lithium polymer battery	PRC

Notes: PRC = People's Republic of China.
[a]For the use of components for Apple's products, see note a of Table 8.1.
[b]Apple has moved away from Samsung Electronics to Elpida for DRAM and Toshiba for the NAND flash memory for the new generations of its products.
[c]As a fabless semiconductor company, Broadcom outsources production to Asian foundries, such as SMIC, TSMC, and UMC.
[d]Infineon has test and assembling facilities in the PRC, Indonesia, Malaysia, and Singapore.
Source: Author's own research.

8.4.2. *Ownership, location, and externalization advantages: A new theoretical paradigm*

According to the Ownership–Location–Internalization (OLI) paradigm (Dunning 1993), FDI takes place when three sets of determining factors exist simultaneously: (i) ownership-specific advantages of an MNC, (ii) location advantages of a host country, and (iii) internalization advantages — benefits in an intra-firm relationship *vis-à-vis* an arm's length relationship. The above discussed pattern in the global electronics industry, as highlighted by the *Fox–Apple* partnership and the associated production network, seems to be determined by the co-existence of the ownership-specific advantages of MNCs (both brand owners and contract manufacturers) and the location advantages of a host country, coupled with a crucial third factor — externalization advantages, namely benefits in contract manufacturing (a specific form of arm's length, inter-firm relationship) compared to an intra-firm relationship. It is the relative (dis)advantage of internalization and externalization that explains why lead firms such as Apple make the strategic choice of international outsourcing, rather than outward FDI, for taking advantage of the low-cost production factors in emerging economies.

From the viewpoint of brand owners, the combination of international outsourcing by themselves and FDI by contract manufacturers offer certain advantages. On the one hand, ownership advantages of contract manufacturers can be leveraged for strengthening those of brand owners. On the other, FDI activities undertaken by contract manufacturers help the brand owners exploit indirectly the location advantages of emerging economies.

8.4.2.1. *Combining ownership advantages*

In the case of the *Fox–Apple* partnership, ownership advantages of Apple are based on its proprietary assets in terms of brands, technologies, innovative capacities, and business strategies. While ownership advantages of Foxconn are reflected in the company's "total cost" solutions, as well as in its unique managerial model and technological capacity. Advantages of Foxconn have complemented those of Apple by offering a manufacturing solution with high efficiency, reliability, and flexibility, which in turn supports Apple's unique business strategy characterized by highly innovative technologies, high-end products, and high-speed product life cycles. In the area of research and development (R&D), Apple's leadership in product innovation and Foxconn's strength in process innovation have been well combined. The complementary nature of the two companies' ownership advantages, coupled with their respective strengths in the different stages of the value chain, provides a basis for the formation of a long-lasting and dominating alliance in the global electronics industry.

8.4.2.2. *Indirectly leveraging location advantages*

As a foreign investor, Foxconn focuses on the PRC in its production location decision because of the country's unique location advantages for efficiency-seeking FDI. These advantages include, for instance, large availability and low cost of production factors (mainly labor and industrial land), good infrastructure, a strong industrial cluster, and a unique policy environment. As the PRC is a country of a continental size, and significant discrepancies exist within the country, the above-mentioned advantages are often available at different locations. For instance, Foxconn's first principal production location in the PRC was at Longhua, Shenzhen, where at the high peak more than 300,000 workers were organized in a massive production campus. As part of a highly concentrated industrial cluster in the Pearl Delta region, a symbol of the PRC's status as the "workshop of the world," the campus was called "Foxconn city." Later, a number of other "Foxconn cities" of similar scale were established in other locations,[16] mostly inland for cost considerations. This shows that, while the low-cost advantage of Shenzhen has disappeared due to rising costs, similar "location advantages" have become available elsewhere thanks to the rapid buildup of infrastructure and formation of industrial clusters inland.

The ability to leverage location advantages in PRC seems to be an important ownership advantage of Foxconn. In this sense, the ownership advantages of foreign investors and the location advantages of host countries have become interlinked. Foxconn's way of manufacturing has brought mass production to new heights. To establish and manage massive production facilities that often involve more than 100,000 workers each is a challenging task, and Foxconn has been able to do it effectively since the early years of its operation in the PRC. Without the support of local governments in terms of land acquisition, workforce recruitment, and various other facilitative roles, this is impossible. Sometimes, the support is rather direct. For instance, the government of Jincheng (Shanxi Province) has provided cash subsidies for each recruited worker in a recent

---

[16]For instance, Foxconn's production facility in Zhengzhou (Henan Province) had recruited 180,000 workers by March 2012. Foxconn's plan in Chengdu (Sichuan Province) had about 164,000 workers by December 2012. Other production facilities for Apple's products are in Chongqing, Wuhan (Hubei Province), Taiyuan (Shanxi Province), etc.

multibillion-dollar investment project of Foxconn. The cooperation of a developmental state at the local level with the MNC is an important feature of the "Chinese model" (Liang 2004) — and the size and experience of Foxconn have given the company a strong leverage in this respect.

8.4.2.3. *Exploiting externalization advantages*

First of all, externalization offers brand owners the possibility to increase flexibility, reduce risk, and enhance competitiveness by transferring low value-added functions, fixed assets, and inventories to contract manufacturers. Theoretically, this is explained by transaction costs economics,[17] particularly in a dynamic industrial context in electronics. The advancement of "general purpose technologies" (especially information and communication technology) has substantially reduced transaction costs and coordination problems, while modularization (as well as other advances in production techniques) has reduced the degree of asset specificity, both of which are in favor of externalization *vis-à-vis* internalization. This is in contrast with the traditional situation where markets for production inputs are imperfect, if they exist at all, and may involve significant transaction costs or time lags (UNCTAD 1998). Indeed, like other brand owners in the electronics industry, Apple finds greater benefits in exploiting its ownership advantages (coupled with Foxconn's advantages) through contract manufacturing arrangements rather than FDI.

Externalization offers another crucial advantage for brand owners to be able to focus on certain areas that they are good at. Along the different stages of the value chain, for instance, Apple can concentrate on product development, brand management, and marketing, while Foxconn takes care of production and assembly. To some extent, the complex and tedious job of supply chain management, parts procurement, and final assembly have been mostly left to Foxconn. With regard to R&D, Apple can focus on product innovation, and the burden of process innovation is on the shoulder of Foxconn.

---

[17]See Williamson (1975, 1983) for related issues such as asset specificity and contractual relationship.

8.5. New Tendencies, Challenges, and Development Consequences

Electronics GVCs have demonstrated tendencies of "polarization" in different areas. First, the production network has shown a strong degree of geographical concentration. Global production networks of many electronics products are not really global, but Asian, with a strong degree of concentration on the PRC. As production costs in the country rise, relocation of manufacturing has been taking place. However, the dominant direction of capital flows has been from coastal regions to inland. Foxconn has established production bases in a diverse range of countries, including Brazil, the Czech Republic, Mexico, and Viet Nam, and may undertake large-scale investments in final assembly facilities in other low-income countries, such as Indonesia. Nevertheless, production activities of the company are still highly concentrated in the PRC. In the meantime, the production of high value-added components has started to relocate to the PRC in a significant manner, which will further strengthen the country's dominant position in the electronics production networks. Upgrading opportunities in industrial clusters vary with the way GVCs are governed (Humphrey and Schmitz 2012). These latest developments in Apple's production networks show that proximity to major markets and customers is still important in firms' location decision and that the concentration of final assembly is likely to be a strong pulling factor for components production.

From a broader perspective, principally only two regions are closely linked to the electronics GVCs: East Asia and North America. The pattern of the production network of Apple's products is in line with the general features summarized in the previous section. In fact, its formation has been based on two building blocks: first, cross-Pacific outsourcing undertaken by Apple; and second, cross-Strait investment undertaken by Foxconn. It has become a symbol of "ChinAmerica" — the invisible hands of GVCs have closely linked the US, the largest industrialized country with the strongest innovation system, and the PRC, the largest emerging economy with the biggest manufacturing base. The former's strengths in basic research, product innovation, and brand management and the latter's advantages in large availability of low cost of labor (both non-skilled labor and engineers), high-quality infrastructure, and strong industrial clusters are combined, which give rise to an industrial and commercial miracle centered around the *Fox–Apple* partnership.

Along the value chain, firms' division of labor between product development and brand management on the one hand and production and assembly on the other hand has been largely strengthened. Competition takes place at the two stages of the value chain, and Apple and Foxconn have been so far the major winners. The other interesting phenomenon is the tendency of polarization at the innovation stage of the value chain. Product and process innovations have been separated, with brand owners focusing on R&D for new products and contract manufacturers focusing on the R&D for production processes. Apple and Foxconn are leaders in the two fronts of technological innovation respectively, forming an "innovation axis" that becomes the driver of the whole value creation network (Figure 8.1).[18] This is different from the conventional understanding that the lead firm is the single driver in the network. Indeed, with a global network of research centers, Foxconn has become the largest innovator in the electronics industry in terms of issued patents,[19] and the total number of its global patent applications has reached over 100,000.

As the various investigative studies illustrate, the scale of value creation and capture at the final assembly stage is very small, limiting economic benefits where such activities take place. In addition, the social and environmental costs of the new model of massive production should not be neglected. From a dynamic viewpoint, positive impacts (such as local learning and upgrading, as well as technological spillovers) have been observed, while the locking in of emerging MNCs at a certain stage of the value chain continues to be a concern. For low-income countries, locations, and firms absent in the picture, linking up to the global production network remains a challenge. For those already in, moving up the value chain and shifting from comparative to competitive advantages may not be an easy task.

---

[18]Foxconn's R&D activities have shown a focus on the production-related fields, such as material sciences, nanotechnology, heat transfer, thermal treatment, optical plating technique, robotics, and advanced manufacturing.

[19]*Electronics & Instruments Patent Scorecard* released by IPIQ in May 2012.

The dominating pattern of production in the global electronics industry, as highlighted by *Fox–Apple* and its related network, is likely to continue. However, it faces challenges from competing firms and models. For instance, in the smartphone segment, Samsung has recently claimed a leading position in terms of market share; and the company's production model is quite different from that of Apple — most components are produced within the firm, so is the final assembly. In the choice between outward FDI and international outsourcing, the former seems to prevail in the case of Samsung. Challenges also come from the new institutional context after the global financial crisis. Rising protectionist policy measures, in both the trade and investment areas, and developed countries' renewed efforts to bring back manufacturing for employment considerations may lead to the reversion of offshoring. This de-globalization trend may not be able to gain strength in the near future, but Apple's recent efforts to bring back the Mac's production to Fremont, California may be an alarming signal.

8.6. Conclusion

The partnership of *Fox–Apple*, a new term introduced in the chapter, represents a crucial part of the global electronics industry. It is the largest "fruit" of the "tree" of global value creation in the industry, and, in the meantime, its growth and maturation have altered the industrial landscape — the technology, products, competitors, and the way global production is organized. Indeed, "global value tree," another new term introduced in the chapter, has become a term better than "global value chain" in reflecting these features.

Following the traditional GVC approach, this chapter started off with an investigation of the inter-firm relationship between Apple as a brand owner and Foxconn as a contract manufacturer. The analysis demonstrates the emergence of a new type of buyer–supplier relationship, as well as a number of new, salient features of GVCs. The results challenge the conventional thinking on production networks and have significant implications for business practice and policy making alike.

By examining the initial formation, gradual evolution, and rapid expansion of the partnership between Apple and Foxconn, the chapter tries to shed light on the question on how foreign direct investment and contract manufacturing have led to the new structural features of GVCs. Similar to the framework of Dunning's OLI paradigm, this chapter presents a theoretical hypothesis based on the simultaneous presence of ownership, location, and externalization advantages. This "OLE" framework explains the pattern of production networks of Apple and many other leading companies in the global electronics industry. It shows that the relative advantage of externalization explains why lead firms make the strategic choice of international outsourcing, rather than outward FDI, for taking advantage of favorable production conditions in emerging economies. By looking beyond FDI and examining its trade-off with outsourcing, this presents a groundbreaking theoretical effort in international business and economics.

This case study approach in building theory needs to be strengthened by future empirical research. Similar studies at firm and industry levels will be particularly useful in identifying new dynamic factors in the global economy and demonstrating how their emergence changes the manner in which value chains are organized and governed across borders.

References*

Curry, J. and M. Kenney. 1999. Beating the Clock: Corporate Responses to Rapid Change in the PC Industry. *California Management Review* 42(1): 8–35.

Davis, T. 1993. Effective Supply Chain Management. *Sloan Management Review* 34: 35–46.

Duhigg, C. and K. Bradsher. 2012. How the US Lost Out on iPhone Work. *The New York Times*, 21 January.

Dunning, J.H. 1993. *Multinational Enterprises and the Global Economy*. Wokingham: Addison-Wesley.

Einhorn, B. 2007. Apple's Chinese Supply Lines. *Business Week*, 8 January.

Foster, W., Z. Cheng, J. Dedrick, and K.L. Kraemer. 2006. Technology and Organizational Factors in the Notebook Industry Supply Chain. The Centre for Strategic Supply Research and the Personal Computing Industry Centre.

Gereffi, G. 1999. International Trade and Industrial Upgrading in the Apparel Commodity Chain. *Journal of International Economics* 48: 37–70.

Gereffi, G. and M. Korzeniewicz (eds.). 1994. *Commodity Chains and Global Capitalism*. Westport: Praeger.

*The Asian Development Bank refers to China by the name People's Republic of China.

Gereffi, G., J. Humphrey, and T. Sturgeon. 2005. The Governance of Global Value Chains. *Review of International Political Economy* 12(1): 78–104.

Humphrey, J. and H. Schmitz. 2012. How Does Insertion in Global Value Chains Affect Upgrading in Industrial Clusters? *Regional Studies* 36(9): 1017–1027.

Knight, G.A. 1997. Emerging Paradigm for International Marketing: The Born Global Firm. Dissertation, Department of Marketing and Supply Chain Management. Michigan State University, Michigan.

Kraemer, K.L., G. Linden, and J. Dedrick. 2011. Capturing Value in Global Networks: Apple's iPad and iPhone. Working Paper, based on support from the Alfred P. Sloan Foundation and the US National Science Foundation, July.

Lee, Q. 2012. Apple, Foxconn and Manufacturing Strategy. Strategos, Inc. June.

Liang, G. 2004. *New Competition: Foreign Direct Investment and Industrial Development in China*. ERIM, Rotterdam: RSM, Erasmus University.

Linden, G., K.L. Kraemer, and J. Dedrick. 2007. Who Captures Value in a Global Innovation System? The Case of Apple's iPod. Irvine, California: Personal Computing Industry Center (PCIC).

OECD and WTO (Organisation for Economic Co-operation and Development and World Trade Organization). 2013. Trade in Value Added: Concepts, Methodologies and Challenges. Joint OECD–WTO Note, January.

Porter, M.E. 1985. *Competitive Advantage*. New York: Free Press.

Skinner, W. 1969. Manufacturing — Missing Link in Corporate Strategy. *Harvard Business Review*, May–June.

Sturgeon, T.J. 2002. Modular Production Networks: A New American Model of Industrial Organization. *Industrial and Corporate Change* 11(3): 451–496.

Sturgeon, T.J. and G. Gereffi. 2009. Measuring Success in the Global Economy: International Trade, Industrial Upgrading and Business Function Outsourcing in Global Value Chains. *Transnational Corporations* 18(2): 1–37.

Sturgeon, T.J. and M. Kawakami. 2010. Global Value Chains in the Electronics Industry: Was the Crisis a Window of Opportunity for Developing Countries? Policy Research Working Paper 5417, Washington DC: The World Bank.

UNCTAD. 1998. *World Investment Report 1998: Trends and Determinants*. Geneva: United Nations.

Williamson, O. 1975. *Markets and Hierarchies*. New York: Free Press.

Williamson, O. 1983. Credible Commitments: Using Hostages to Support Exchange. *American Economic Review* 73(4): 519–540.

Xing, Y. and N. Detert. 2010. How the iPhone Widens the United States Trade Deficit with the People's Republic of China. ADBI Working Paper No. 257. Tokyo: Asian Development Bank Institute.

Printed in the United States
By Bookmasters